When the Caffeine Wears Off

When the Caffeine Wears Off

De-Hyping the New Economy

Brian Ross

Writers Club Press
San Jose New York Lincoln Shanghai

When the Caffeine Wears Off
De-Hyping the New Economy

Writers Club Press
an imprint of iUniverse.com, Inc.

For information address:
iUniverse.com, Inc.
5220 S 16th, Ste. 200
Lincoln, NE 68512
www.iuniverse.com

The events portrayed in this book are drawn from the author's actual
experiences, but the names of people, companies, products and Web sites are
fictional. Any resemblance to real names is purely coincidental. Likewise, deal
terms and other confidential or identifying information have been disguised.

ISBN: 0-595-18350-6

Printed in the United States of America

For Fred, Sarah and David

CONTENTS

PREFACE

In the fall of 1999, the frenzy surrounding the Internet and the New Economy was reaching a fever pitch. Every day, a handful of dot-coms and other Internet-related companies went public. And once they did, look out. Their valuations surged upward to dizzying levels. For a business even remotely associated with the Net, the world was indeed its oyster.

At the same time this nonsense was occurring, I accepted a job with my Old Economy firm's newly established e-commerce team. As such, I was privileged to have a front row view of the action.

Previously, all I knew about dot-coms and the New Economy was what I read in the newspaper. Soon after I started my assignment, however, it became clear that my daily experiences didn't exactly match what the mainstream press reported. In an attempt to balance the popular perception of the firms and people who populate the New Economy, I wrote this book.

Here, you'll get an insider's view of what really went on behind the scenes during a twelve-month period starting in August 1999. It's written from the perspective of someone working at an established Old Economy company—a firm that's struggling to understand the Internet and its implications. Hence, you'll also get a look at how Corporate America generally operates.

This book is written for those who want to better understand the true workings of the New Economy. I've structured the language so that the subject matter is accessible to a wide audience, regardless of whether the reader has a business background or not.

The book is organized into four sections, which contain a collection of stories and commentary about my experiences. Section One, "In the Beginning…," describes how my firm established its e-commerce effort and how I joined the team. Section Two, "True Stories from the Trenches," shows you how the players in the New Economy really operate behind closed doors. Section Three, "All about New Economy Firms," explains everything you need to know about Internet companies. The final section, "Everything Old is New Again," provides guidance for Old Economy firms wishing to secure a competitive advantage in the New Economy. All four sections will be helpful for Internet-related companies wanting to do business in the post dot-com era.

As you read the pages ahead, you'll discover that this is not your typical "how-to" business book. Nor is it a corporate drama. Instead, think of it as an extended case study. Like a Business School case, Sections One and Two are written in a narrative style and take the reader on a journey. Unlike a B-School case, the book continues on to share observations and lessons learned. These are found in Sections Three and Four. This approach, I believe, will enable the reader to internalize the concepts most effectively and then apply them to his or her own situation.

My goal in writing this book is to make you better informed of the prevailing business practices found in the New Economy. Although I am critical of these practices, please do not interpret this to mean that I am anti-technology. In fact, I am an advocate of technology.

Throughout history, technological advances have enabled mankind to conduct business more efficiently and profitably. But are we really in a "New Economy" where the basic laws of business no longer apply? I think not. From where I sit, the concept of profitability has not been repealed. A firm still needs to have more money in the cash register at the end of the day than it started with or it won't be in business for long.

Put another way, a bad business idea is still a bad business idea—regardless of whether we're talking about a brick-and-mortar company or a dot-com.

One final note. The names of individuals, companies, deal terms and other confidential or identifying information have been disguised. The stories, however, are all true.

ACKNOWLEDGEMENTS

Thank you to Sterling and Sue Ament, Milton and Yvonne Datta, Heidi Newman, Maura O'Neil, Joel Rubenstein, Saul Rubenstein and Faye and Stan Yates who read various drafts and provided comments from a layperson's perspective. Thanks, also, to Maxine Lancaster, Gerald Hogan, Dan-the-Man Bosley and several other Frederick Gold, Inc., employees who read the manuscript and provided comments from a businessperson's perspective. Special thanks to Andrea Dixon, Ph.D., Matthew Johnson and Fred and Sarah Ross who provided not only encouragement and support but also words of wisdom when the going got tough. This book would not have been possible without you.

SECTION ONE:
IN THE BEGINNING

CHAPTER 1
PREACHER MAN

Timing is everything. The man on stage clearly understood this. It had been nearly a minute since he was introduced and the polite applause had faded. The only sound now filling the hushed corporate auditorium was the man's footsteps as he paced back and forth. Every few seconds he slowly nodded his head and looked at the two hundred people assembled before him. His face betrayed only the faintest hint of a smile.

Some in the crowd began to get nervous and shifted in their seats. Others started to giggle. Just then, the man strode over to the lectern, where an unopened bottle of water awaited him. He reached for the bottle, twisted off the top and took a long swig. As he screwed the cap back on, he spoke his first words.

"This is quite a turnout. Either you're all excited—or scared."

A burst of nervous laughter erupted from the standing room-only gathering. We were, in fact, excited *and* scared. After all, the person before us was billed as an expert on the Internet and the New Economy—both of which were getting a great deal of attention in August 1999.

The speaker smiled broadly, placed the water bottle back on the lectern and started across the stage with a vengeance.

"If you ever want to see real estate inflation, look to the Internet," he said quickly. "If you don't grab Internet real estate while it's cheap, it will go up exponentially. I think this will happen every six months."

He paused for a brief second to let this sink in. Then he turned and walked briskly to the other side of the stage, where he started a passionate discourse about the Internet. As he spoke, he gestured emphatically with his hands and arms. He looked like a minister on late-night cable TV.

For the next 20 minutes, he went on about the Internet and how it was the salvation for an Old Economy company such as ours. The message of his sermon was that "the Internet changes everything." We listened with rapt attention. No one dared say a word.

Suddenly, the Preacher Man stopped dead in his tracks and just looked at us. He had been moving and talking nonstop for some time. Now, he appeared dismayed, almost angry. His expression seemed to say, "You just don't get it, do you?"

There were large beads of sweat on his brow. He reached into his suit pocket for a handkerchief. As he wiped his face, he spoke to us for the first time slowly and quietly.

"Many of your competitors are ahead of you. You're below the median."

An audible gasp went up from several people. Here we were, Preacher Man's new congregation, and we apparently didn't grasp the sanctity of the Net. In his mind, we were akin to sinners who would burn in Hell when our shareholders asked us why we'd missed the New Economy. If this didn't instill the fear of God in us, nothing would.

But redemption was ours, Preacher Man said, if only we listened to him and his ideas. Suddenly, people sat up in their seats and began taking copious notes. He was now speaking to the converted.

Once more, he began walking from one side of the stage to the other, gesturing wildly and speaking quickly. His next topic was how to work with dot-coms and other Internet-related businesses.

"Welcome these guys when they come in," he implored, holding his arms outstretched as though greeting a long lost friend. "Because when they come in early, they're hungry. They're desperate. And you know what? You don't need to pay anything. *Just give them your content.*"

People scribbled furiously on their notepads and Palm Pilots, hanging on every word. Yes, we were beginning to see the light.

"You need to act on this information, otherwise, my job's not done," said Preacher Man. He then concluded his talk by solemnly assuring us that if we didn't follow his guidance, "you won't even know what hit you."

With that, the assembled masses leapt to their feet and gave the speaker a thunderous round of applause. Moments later, he was surrounded by a dozen souls clamoring for just one more piece of wisdom. I didn't stay to listen. My head was spinning. I found it difficult to make sense of everything I'd just heard. In fact, I wasn't exactly sure if I'd just been listening to God or the Devil himself.

As I walked back to my office, my anxiety grew. Much of what the speaker said didn't seem to make sense. For example, while I agreed that we shouldn't pay money to some start-up dot-com that approached us, I couldn't justify why we should just give them our content for their own Web sites. Surely our content—meaning the information that our company had developed around its products and services—had a value associated with it. Why would we just give it away? Shouldn't we get something in return? This question was never answered.

Once back at my desk, I looked over my notes. At one point Preacher Man told us, "don't drive people from your Web site." Then, a few minutes later, he commanded us to "partner with other sites to direct visitors from your Web site to theirs." This was a direct contradiction. He spoke so fast and with such conviction, however, that I didn't catch this when he first said it. Apparently, no one else did, either.

Although I was becoming increasingly skeptical of what I had just heard, I was troubled by one thought: What if Preacher Man really did understand the New Economy? Sure, much of what he said wasn't exactly plausible, but it wasn't beyond a reasonable doubt. What if we really didn't "get it" but our competition did? What if, as absurd as it sounded, that "not this year, not next year, but maybe the year after that, people will give away cars" to capitalize on selling Internet-related services, such as restaurant finders, to a captive audience? What if...?

Little did I know that these questions would keep me awake late at night in the months ahead. But on this fine August day, my thoughts were on other matters. Someone else at the company—not a mere associate-level individual such as myself—could grapple with these issues.

Unfortunately, my smugness didn't last long. Less than a week later, I received a phone call that literally changed my life. As it turned out, Preacher Man was the first of many New Economy disciples who would make the pilgrimage to my doorstep.

CHAPTER 2
THE PHONE CALL

"Are you working hard?" the caller wanted to know.

"Of course," I said, "I always work hard."

"Well, get ready to work harder."

And with those words, my career in e-commerce began.

The date was August 8, 1999 and this was no ordinary conversation. The person phoning was Maxine Lancaster, the highly regarded vice president of worldwide marketing at my company. Maxine was calling to offer me a job as a founding member of our new Global e-Commerce group. I was stunned.

But the good news didn't stop there. In addition, I was to be promoted from an associate-level position into management. My new title: Global e-Commerce Manager. My life had suddenly gotten a whole lot better.

At a Fortune 500 company like mine, a promotion to management is a significant achievement. There is no job title inflation at Frederick Gold, Inc., a century-old firm, which creates products for the medical industry. It generally took two to five years of exemplary leadership and performance before one would even be considered for a management position. When the time was right, our Management Selection Committee rendered a decision—up or out. In many ways, it was similar to being inducted into a fraternity.

My name had come before the selection committee in May and I had the good fortune of being placed on the "manager-ready" list. This meant that I was available to discuss any management offer that came my way. Maxine Lancaster had just tendered such an offer.

After four years with the company, I was about to see a substantial change in my compensation. In addition to a generous benefits package and base salary, there would be stock options and annual performance awards, provided our company met its goals. For the first time in my life, money would not be an issue.

In my earlier days, prior to returning for my MBA, I had struggled to make a living. My undergraduate degree was in film and television production. For me, it wasn't the path to fame and fortune. Although I worked in Hollywood for a few years, I led a feast or famine existence. My experience in tinsel town is not something that I fondly remember.

A steady diet of ramen noodles and tuna sandwiches was enough to convince me I needed to select another career—one that offered a stable paycheck. However, I wanted to do something where I could still be creative and entrepreneurial. Surprisingly, Corporate America provided the answer.

When I first interviewed with Frederick Gold during business school, the recruiter told me that the firm was looking for people who would be "change agents." In other words, folks with unique life experiences who could come in, take some risks and challenge the status quo. Given my previous work experience in the film business, which was definitely unique as compared to the standards of most industries, this was a challenge I couldn't pass up. I joined the company straight out of business school.

After successful stints in sales, operations and strategy, I could think of no better place to be a change agent than as an initial member of our e-commerce team. The opportunity to make a difference seemed enormous. So much, in fact, that I accepted the position instantly when Maxine offered it to me. I was so caught up in the moment and thinking about future possibilities that I didn't ask some obvious questions, such as how many associates would be reporting to me.

Maxine, a petite woman raised on a Montana ranch, was known for telling great tales. On this day, however, she was getting right down to business. My assignment, she said, would start immediately. The decision for our company to enter into the e-commerce arena was coming from the highest levels of the organization. Maxine and our Chief Technology Officer would be the sponsors of the e-commerce group.

Our department was to be small, no more than seven people initially. This seemed a little surprising, given that there were over 20,000 employees worldwide at our company. I suppose the reason for this was that if the experiment didn't work out, the seven of us could go back to our previous jobs and there would be little disruption to the organization.

In addition to me, the group would consist of a director, five other managers and an administrative assistant. Our director, Gerald Hogan, from Australia, was an outside hire with significant e-commerce experience in another industry. By outside hire, I mean that he had never worked with our company before. This was a significant departure from the norm, but it was a realization that true e-commerce expertise did not exist at our firm. Gerald had accepted his position just moments before Maxine placed her call to me. I was the second person hired on the team.

My job, as I understood it, had three components. First, I was to find and negotiate with dot-coms and other New Economy companies for services that would give Frederick Gold a presence on the Internet. Second, I was to assist in the implementation of our e-commerce strategy. Third, I was to focus on mapping out the e-commerce environment as it related specifically to our industry and our competitors. It would be a lot of work for one person to do, let alone do well. In hindsight, it was an impossible workload.

A fair question to ask is what e-commerce experience I had to justify my being offered such a position. The short answer is not a whole lot, but probably more than most people at my company. What I did have, however, was a strong desire to learn and plenty of relevant industry knowledge. In my previous assignment, I was responsible for forecasting how the health care industry would look in three to five years.

As part of this work, I began to do extensive research in the evenings and weekends on the evolving nature of e-commerce. I wrote some white papers on the topic, spoke with various individuals at other companies and even visited some firms on the West Coast. What I did was not out of the ordinary. Anyone could have done it if they had taken the time. But they didn't. So, I became a de facto expert on e-commerce at Frederick Gold, Inc.

It turned out that one of my white papers made its way up to our Chief Technology Officer, Russell Dunn. Russell was a big man with a friendly smile. He apparently liked what he read and made a mental note to keep track of me. I didn't know it, but as plans for the e-commerce group were being made, there was already one person who was interested in seeing me be one of the initial members.

When my brief call with Maxine ended, I was grinning from ear to ear. Talk about a plum assignment! My mind was running through scenario after scenario of what I needed to do over the next several weeks. After four years of long hours, I was about to engage in something quite sexy and high profile. And the title, "Global e-Commerce Manager," who could ask for anything better, save for, perhaps, Fighter Pilot?

And yet, for all the joy I was feeling, there was something stuck deep in my mind that kept playing itself over and over. "Get ready to work harder. Get ready to work harder…." I didn't know it at the time, but Maxine's words were going to be strangely prophetic over the next twelve months.

CHAPTER 3
NOW WHAT?

Shortly after the Maxine Lancaster call, I was packing up my belongings and moving from my old office into our corporate center campus, with its covered parking and significantly better food. Even my cubicle, although no larger than my previous one, somehow seemed more spacious.

A couple days later, the third member of our group was named. Anna Alvarez came to us from our Mexican affiliate. She was tall, dark-skinned and had long black hair. I heard her once say of herself that she looked like Pocahontas. An impressive woman, she had solid business and computer systems experience. To top it off, she had also lived in several countries around the world and spoke, I think, four or five languages. She had only been in the States for about eight weeks, so this was an experience for her, indeed.

The first task Anna and I had was to develop the e-commerce group's budget. We got this assignment because Gerald Hogan, the newly hired director, was wrapping things up overseas and had not yet started work with us. Luckily, I had created the initial budget for our Northeast Area two years ago, so the budgeting process wasn't new to me.

Anna and I decided to split up the task. Given her background, she would calculate the IT components of the budget; I would take care of the other elements. One of these was headcount. Surely we would have more people in our department in Year 2000 as a result of our projects being successful. Of course, this begged the question, "what projects would we undertake?" In essence, we were designing a budget without knowing exactly for what purpose.

I spoke with Maxine Lancaster and asked how many associates I would have. Maxine's answer was to budget for one person in 2000. This meant that I would be a manager for the five remaining months in 1999, yet not have anyone directly reporting to me. It also meant that come 2000, I would only have one associate. Somehow, I'd envisioned at least two to three associate-level individuals on my team, given the amount of work that needed to be done. Oh well, that's what I get for not asking the question earlier.

More importantly, I began to realize that I wasn't sure what to budget for when it came to the projects we would undertake. In fact, I didn't really know what our e-commerce objective and strategy was. Oh, sure, I had a vague sense of it from my call a few days prior when I accepted my position, but I didn't have the specifics. I took it on faith that there was a strategy. Why else would the decision be made to start a new group and devote budget, headcount and other scarce resources if there was no clearly defined strategy?

I asked Anna if she knew the strategy. As we spoke, it became clear that she didn't have any more knowledge on the topic than I, except that she did have a three-page memo from Russell Dunn, the CTO and a personal friend of hers. The document contained his thoughts for the department. She let me look at the pages, but swore me to secrecy.

The document wasn't terribly helpful, but it did contain brief job descriptions for each of the people in our group. As it turned out, this would be the first—and only—time that I saw a written description for my job. It wasn't exactly what Maxine Lancaster described on the phone, but I decided that my job would be what Maxine had conveyed because it sounded more challenging.

After spending a couple more days trying to develop the budget, I became frustrated that I didn't have a full picture of what was expected of me. Yes, I'd signed on to this new endeavor without being forced to do so, knowing full well that there would be a certain level of ambiguity associated with it. But now it was getting ridiculous. Even Anna was feeling unhappy about our predicament. We decided that we had spent long enough in the dark. If there was an e-commerce strategy for our group to implement, we wanted to know it. So Anna contacted Russell, her patron saint, and I contacted Maxine to arrange a time when we could discuss the strategy. In this way, we'd double up on the two people championing the effort.

A couple days went by and we heard nothing. This was unusual. We began to panic. Had we done something wrong by contacting Maxine and Russell? Of course not. Anybody would want to know what it is they're being asked to do.

On the third day, both Anna and I received phone calls informing us to meet Maxine and Russell at six that evening for dinner at Ruth's Chris Steakhouse. At that time, we were told, we would learn our mission.

Looking back, this was to be the first of many meals at steakhouses around the country. I'm not sure why, but almost everyone I deal with in the New Economy wants to eat steak. Go figure. All I know is that in the last twelve months, I've eaten more beef than in the last ten years combined.

After work, Anna and I drove to the restaurant. We arrived right on time at the downtown Ruth's Chris. We announced ourselves to the hostess and asked if Maxine or Russell had arrived. A quick check of the reservation list found no mention of them. How could that be? Then it dawned on us. There was another Ruth's Chris way down on the south side of town. It was at least a thirty-minute drive at this time of day. The location of the Ruth's Chris we were now standing in was only minutes from our office. Was it possible that they meant the other restaurant and had neglected to tell us? We asked the hostess to call the other branch to inquire. Sure enough, the two were down there waiting for us.

When Anna and I arrived forty-five minutes later, we were led to a private room in the back where Maxine and Russell were enjoying some beers. They greeted us and we all sat down for drinks and small talk. After the appetizers arrived, Maxine pulled out three unmarked notebooks and handed one to each of us. Over the next few hours, we went into detail on the e-commerce strategy. Thankfully, there was a strategy and it made sense, especially since it fit nicely into our company's overall business strategy.

By the end of the evening, I was back to feeling better about my decision to join the e-commerce group. Given what we now knew, Anna and I could complete the budget, albeit at a cursory level.

Russell closed out the evening by telling us that a group of consultants would be brought in to help us develop three e-commerce pilot programs. The goal of each pilot, which would be carried out in the months ahead, was to explore a different element of our strategy. Maxine noted that by doing this our learning would be more robust than if we had all three pilots focused on the exact same issue.

In a few days, the consultants would arrive in town. I was asked to work closely with them. "Help them get the necessary background information compiled from different parts of the company," I was told.

I had never worked directly with consultants before, but given the stories I'd heard from other people and my own experience with business school classmates who eventually became consultants, I wasn't exactly looking forward to the experience.

On top of overseeing the consultants, I also had responsibility for completing my portion of the budget. Indeed, I was beginning to "work harder," just as Maxine had assured me two weeks before.

CHAPTER 4
LET THE GAMES BEGIN

The budget work proceeded on course, aided in part by Anna being moved to the cubicle next to me. This made communicating with one another much easier. Until now, Anna had been located in a different building, waiting for space near me to became available.

A day after Anna changed cubicles, the consultants arrived. It seemed strange that the consulting firm selected wasn't exactly known for its e-commerce prowess. The mystery was solved when I learned the accounting arm of the same firm also did our books. Apparently, the reasoning was "if they're good at accounting, they must be good at consulting." It was bad logic.

During my first meeting with the consultants, Anton, the project leader, asked if we had any data about e-commerce and our industry that we could share with them. I was a little puzzled. Wouldn't these folks have their own data that they would share with us? After all, they were consultants and we were paying them. Yes, I had plenty of data—all the stuff I'd spent my evenings and weekends compiling a few months earlier on my last job. I wasn't all that excited about just giving it to someone else outside our company. My fear was that it would cease to be my information and instead become something that the consultants would claim as being their own.

I called Maxine and expressed my concern. "If I give them my data," I said, "then why are we paying them?" Maxine's answer was to provide them with the data and not to worry about it. I complied.

The consultants also wanted to speak with various individuals at our company about their thoughts on e-commerce. For the next few days, I worked to set up interviews with several people. It was now becoming quite clear to me how consultants—at least how this particular group of consultants—worked. First, they would take existing information, put it into a new presentation and label it as their own research. Next, they would interview various people and then parrot back the findings in their recommendations.

The whole thing made no sense. This didn't seem to be "consulting" so much as it was "compiling" and "regurgitating."

Sure enough, when I saw the first set of slides from the consultants, my work was identified as "Big Head Consultants Research." I was livid. "If you're going to label it as yours, then do your own research," I told them. "Otherwise, identify it as 'research provided by the client.'" They did so, but reluctantly.

When they finally did do a little of their own research, it was woefully inadequate. In some instances, it was flat out wrong. Even after this was pointed out to them—and supported by fact—they still refused to change their findings. I soon realized that we were paying a lot of money to train a group of people fresh-out-of-school. Weren't they supposed to be bringing us some expertise? In fact, they knew little about our industry.

As our relationship with them began to sour, there was one crowning blow. I had recently obtained a thick binder with extremely confidential information regarding the redesign for one of our Web sites. The binder had several pages of research on our brand strategy and how our new Web site would assist in fulfilling the strategy. There were perhaps five of these binders in existence.

When the consultants learned that I had a copy, they wanted it. I hesitated, but eventually provided it to them. As I handed the binder to Anton, I told him, "The information contained in this is confidential. Don't let it out of your sight."

"I won't," he assured me. It was a Friday evening and I would have the binder back first thing on Monday morning.

On Sunday evening, Anton left me the following voicemail:

"I've got some bad news for you. I gave the binder to Suzie at the airport in D.C. You know Suzie; she's one of the people on my team. Anyway, when Suzie arrived at her apartment in Georgetown, she realized that she didn't have the binder. She thinks she left it on the back seat of the taxi. She's called the cab company to inquire. But let's be honest, if she left it there, the chances of us getting it back are very slim. So I'd like to get another binder. Thanks."

That was the entire message. There was no apology or indication of remorse. Talk about hubris. If Anton honestly thought a second copy was really going to make its way to him, he was smoking dope. My firm has competitors in the Washington, D.C. area. If this binder fell into their hands, it would be a significant breach of security.

My response to Anton when I spoke live with him on Monday was terse: "Find the damn binder."

"What about a second copy?"

"Listen, I trusted you with the first binder. You told me you wouldn't let it out of your sight, and you gave it to Suzie. For crying out loud, she's just out of college and working her first real job. What sort of an idiot does that? There's not going to be a second binder, just find the first one. And until you find that binder, there won't be any more data shared with you."

During my adult life, it was rare that I lost my temper. Unfortunately, this was the first of many times over the coming months that I would become enraged.

Miraculously, a few days later, the missing binder appeared. It turned out that the cab driver was an honest man who reported the misplaced binder to his company and returned it at the end of his shift. Thank goodness. "All's well that ends well," Anton said when he handed the binder to me.

Around this time, Gerald Hogan, the e-commerce team's director and my boss, moved to the States and began working with us. Gerald was a welcome addition to the team. He spoke in a relaxed Aussie accent and had a wickedly dry sense of humor. An incredibly smart man, Gerald could quickly read people and situations. For example, a few days after he started, we were meeting with the consultants when he noticed a stack of documents near Anton. When Gerald asked to see them, Anton glanced at his colleagues and then slid the stack across the table to him. It turned out that these were "best practice" memos the consulting firm had collected from previous engagements and research.

Although I dislike consultants, I must admit that one thing they do well is to share information among themselves. If any company in Corporate America did this only half as well as the consultants do, it would enjoy a significant competitive advantage by being able to make well-informed decisions quickly. I imagine the research that I provided to the consultants has probably joined their "best practices" repository.

Once Gerald understood what the documents contained, he asked if we could copy them. It was information that would be of value to our company.

"I don't know," Anton stammered. "These are originals and it's very important information."

"Don't worry," Gerald smiled, "We can go upstairs and run copies of these right now."

"I don't know…"

I couldn't resist the opportunity that had just presented itself.

"Hey," I chimed in, "Those are very important documents, aren't they?"

"Yes," Anton answered, somewhat annoyed.

"And you don't want to let them out of your sight, do you?"

"I just said they were important."

"I understand. Kind of like that binder I gave you a few weeks ago, huh?"

Ah, the famous binder. There was complete silence. Within minutes the meeting ended and we were heading upstairs to a photocopy machine. On the way up, Anton turned to me and said in a voice only loud enough for me to hear, "You just won't let that binder thing rest, will you?"

"All's well that ends well," I replied.

CHAPTER 5
BUILDING CONSENSUS

I was in my job less than four weeks by this point when I began to notice changes about myself. In addition to developing a quick temper, I wasn't sleeping well. Insomnia, which I had never really had before, was becoming a nightly phenomenon. I was also working some very long hours, which meant that my life outside of work was falling apart. While most everyone else at the office was doing the eight-to-five routine, I was getting in around 7:00 a.m. and staying late into the evening. There was simply too much work to do and I didn't have anyone I could delegate to.

Around this time, Russell Dunn paid me a late night visit at my desk. Talk about a heady experience. Here I was, a virtual nobody, and the CTO is coming to ask how it's going. I like Russell. It's clear how he got to where he is. He sincerely cares about others and doing what's right. This visit was just another example of that. So it was that just the two of us were kicking back at my cubicle at eight in the evening while the cleaning crew vacuumed around us.

We talked about the future of e-commerce and what it would mean to our company. At one point during the conversation, Russell said that if the effort didn't pay off, we would have no trouble getting jobs at other companies.

This wasn't exactly comforting. In fact, it was the first time I'd ever heard such a comment from someone at my firm. Most employees at

Frederick Gold have worked there for 20 to 30 years. I, too, had visions of staying with the firm for the long run. I liked the people and the business. More importantly, I felt that I was being rewarded for my performance and not how I dressed.

Russell's visit was the first of many I would have with different people around the company. Prior to my joining the e-commerce group, people weren't exactly lining up to talk with me. Now, it seemed as though every one of the company's 20,000 employees wanted to meet me. My calendar was out of control. Meetings and lunches were being scheduled with abandon. Everyone wanted to know what our strategy was or to tell me what they thought it should be. Lots of people had an opinion on the subject and they wanted to be heard.

Why didn't they go to Gerald Hogan, my director? I suppose people just felt more comfortable coming to me—perhaps since I wasn't an "outsider." In time, however, Gerald had his fair share of "get-to-know-you" meetings.

As mentioned previously, ours was a small group. At this time, Gerald, Anna and I constituted the e-commerce department. The organizational structure was unusually simple. Anna and I reported to Gerald. Gerald, in turn, reported to Maxine Lancaster, the worldwide marketing vice president. Gerald also had a dotted line reporting relationship with Russell. Although both Maxine and Russell were the corporate sponsors, or champions, of the e-commerce group, we belonged to the corporate marketing organization, not information technology. Given the philosophical differences regarding business and new technologies that existed between us marketing folks and our IT counterparts, this seemed like a rational decision, but one that many in the IT department vehemently disagreed with. As it turned out, they weren't the only ones questioning the validity of our team.

Our company is a large organization and building consensus around a new idea is incredibly important. The primary reason many newly formed groups had a tough time was due to a lack of organizational buy-in. As such, we needed to gain support early on for our group and the strategy we hoped to implement. This support would be necessary from key people around the company. Luckily, Maxine and Russell had a plan.

In late July, a few days prior to accepting my new position, I was invited to Tampa for a covert meeting with a handful of influential people at Frederick Gold. The same consulting company that would be officially hired two weeks later to help launch our effort was in charge of facilitating this summit.

The meeting was an example of what Maxine and Russell hoped to accomplish on a much larger scale four weeks later when about 75 people from our company would meet over a three-day period in Denver to build consensus for our e-commerce strategy and select our pilot programs.

The Tampa Meeting was my first extended opportunity to meet face-to-face with people who had close ties to Silicon Valley. One of these people, whom we nicknamed Yoda, served as a perfect representative for the Valley Folk. He was a brilliant, rapacious capitalist who had made millions over the years working with some well-known technology companies. He also looked the part of wealthy Valley Geek, with his long pony tail, black-framed glasses and matching black coat, shoes and slacks.

At one point, the topic of health care in the United States came up. This subject is of critical interest to my company. As we know from the current bickering in Washington and elsewhere, there are no easy answers when it comes to health care—unless, of course, you're a consultant.

At one point, I asked Yoda, "Do you think health care is a right or a privilege?" This is a key question, for its answer determines how a society will care for its people. I don't think it's clearly answered right now in the United States. Well, it apparently stumped Yoda, too, for a moment. He considered the question and then said, "I work hard for my money. I can afford to pay for my health care and for that of my family. If people can't pay for their own health care, well, that's too bad."

"But what if your son or daughter is born with a terrible condition that requires constant and expensive care?" I challenged.

"I can pay for it."

"OK, but what about someone who's doing all he can to support his family and then one day his kid is struck by a drunk driver and paralyzed? What if he can't pay the hundreds of thousands of dollars for care that this kid is going to need over his lifetime?"

"Too bad."

Yoda's answer made many at my company more than a little uneasy. Shortly thereafter, he left the meeting and headed back to Seattle, where, he said, he had to see the "evil folks" in Redmond. It was a blatant reference to Microsoft.

When all was said and done, the Tampa Meeting was little more than a brainstorming session in a cool-looking room. Aside from that, however, I'm not sure the consultants helped us leave with any more than we came in with.

The Denver Meeting was to be a different story. Here, we would all work together—all the disparate factions within our company, and the consultants—to flesh out the strategy and then decide which three projects to implement. Three somehow being the chosen number, given our resources.

A funny thing happened, though, in the days leading up to Denver. For a variety of reasons, certain groups of invited individuals declined to attend. The most obvious absentees would be key members from our U.S. division. The division's president, one of the highest-ranking people at our company, and his lieutenant in charge of strategy both would be no-shows.

I was concerned. Prior to my promotion, I had spent my entire career in the U.S. division and knew there was no love lost between it and our corporate group. In fact, the division viewed the corporate folks as incompetents who were nothing but overhead—the sort of people who liked to indulge in endless meetings. In turn, the corporate people saw the U.S. division as always wanting to do things its own way. Sadly, there was some degree of truth to how each group viewed the other.

One of the reasons that I moved out of the U.S. division and accepted the job in corporate is that I honestly—and naively—believed I would be able to help close the gap between the U.S. division and corporate, given my network of contacts in the U.S. Unfortunately, I soon learned this wasn't to be the case.

It was widely known that the president of the U.S. division had a fondness for technology and wanted to start his own Internet Center of Excellence. The Global e-Commerce group, which Maxine and Russell were championing, thus appeared to steal the president's thunder. He had wanted to see such a group housed in his division. It seemed to me that the stage was being set for yet another political battle. By not attending the meeting, I believed the U.S. division's president was signaling that he had better things to do than be there for our team.

Whether or not the top folks in the U.S. division supported the Global e-Commerce group is a question that will go unanswered. Several key people from the division did attend the meeting, but the absence of the president and his chief strategist was duly noted.

During the grueling three-day session in Denver, there was great debate. An objective observer might have instead described the session as a "great argument." Many in the group felt that the expertise for a venture into e-commerce didn't exist at an "Old Economy" firm such as ours and that we'd be better off hiring people from the outside. When it was explained that we'd done just that with Gerald Hogan, the response was that we needed even more help from the outside—although it was clear that the issue was more of a smokescreen than anything else.

Others felt the outcome of the meeting was predetermined from the beginning. By this they meant that the strategy and the three pilot projects to be implemented had long been decided and this was just an exercise in rubber-stamping. To some extent, I must admit that I agree with this view. Again, because many of the people attending the meeting felt that their input was not taken seriously, there was not a true building of consensus. This meant that there would not be critical support when it was needed in the coming months.

Additionally, the question of governance and accountability was not adequately addressed. Although people at the executive level of the company supported the outcome of the meeting, the everyday rank-and-file—the frontline managers and directors who are actually responsible for getting things done—did not. Without accountability or penalties for withholding support, they would be blameless if they chose to focus on other, "more important" tasks.

Of course, hindsight is 20/20. At the time, I thought the Denver Meeting was fairly successful. Looking back, it's clear to me the meeting was anything but. The seeds for what was about to come were sown during the three days that the 75 of us met. Had everyone who attended truly felt his voice was heard, we wouldn't have had nearly the issues that cropped up with annoying regularity over the coming weeks.

Regardless, we now had a confirmed strategy, although not necessarily the support for it. We also had our three pilot programs chosen: one in Brazil and two in the United States. Anna would oversee the Brazilian project, which was to test if consumers would order our products over the Internet. The two U.S. pilots were to focus on the development of interactive Web sites for our two biggest brands. Since I had helped work on the budgeting, I knew there was plenty of money dedicated to these pilots. We may have lacked headcount, but we certainly didn't lack dollars. This was a change from my past assignments, where I nearly had to ask permission to receive an extra pad of paper.

There was one other event in Denver worth noting. This was a dinner that occurred on the first night of the meeting. There were eight of us, including Anna and me. All of the attendees had very successful careers with the company. We enjoyed a great meal of Chinese food while seated around a large circular table. As we were cracking open our fortune cookies, one of the men began holding court about his career and all the possessions—the motorcycles, the sports cars, and so forth—that he had accumulated over the years as a result of his hard work. His conclusion was that it was all worth it.

One of the other people at the table took a final sip of his beer and said, "Bob, if I'm not mistaken, you're on your second marriage." It was true, Bob noted without rancor, and then added "if *I'm* not mistaken, Joe, you're also on your second marriage." Joe nodded and then looked directly to his right, where Tim was sitting. Tim said, "Actually, I'm happily married and we just had our first child." And so it went, going around the table, person by person, with all the attendees stating whether they were divorced. It was like a strange poker game where everyone was anteing up. Of all the married people who had responded thus far, everyone—except Tim—had been divorced.

They skipped over Anna and me because we were both single. But sitting between us was Fred. He'd been quiet during the entire conversation, which wasn't unusual. Fred was always pretty quiet. Coincidentally, he had also been Anna's boss earlier in her career. Now it was Fred's turn to answer. I looked at him. His eyes were filling with tears. I knew from one of my "get-to-know-you meetings" just a couple weeks before that he was married and had three kids. Fred never looked up from his plate. "I'm separated," he said in a weak voice before raising a glass of water to his mouth.

Fred was the last to speak. An awkward silence followed. Anna and I looked at one another. It's hard to know which of us was more shaken. Later, as I walked with her back to the hotel, I vowed that I was going to reprioritize my life outside of work. Sure, the job was important. Of course it was high profile. But there was no way in hell I was going to end up like these guys. No way.

In September 1999, as I entered my second full month in my new job, I was certain of three things:

I would play a key role in moving our 100-year-old firm into the New Economy.

I was going to regain control of my social life.

I would be finished with consultants.

Section Two:
True Stories from the Trenches

CHAPTER 6
COCKROACHES

When I returned from Denver, my marching orders were clear: Go forth and implement. But first, the budget had to be completed, which we did early in September. Next, the human resources department finally got moving and approved three additional members for our team.

Our new colleagues were Brad Whittle, Donald Rawlings and Allen Ackerman. Brad and Donald, like Anna, would be project leaders, except they were responsible for the two pilot projects based in the United States. The third inductee, Allen, came from our IT group and would be our resident "techie." His job was to serve as a liaison to the IT department. He would assist the marketing people in working through all the various technical issues that were to arise.

Our administrative assistant, Virginia Hartson, joined us near the end of the month. As it turned out, she would be the final person to join the team during our first year. There would be no associates.

All in all, it was a very interesting group of people. We had different backgrounds, came from different parts of the world and had fairly strong, distinct personalities. It was truly a diverse collection of characters. We did, however, have one thing in common: A passion for making the e-commerce experiment work. This turned out to be necessary in the following months, when we'd need all the camaraderie we could muster.

One of my first goals after Denver was to build a database for the universe of e-commerce vendors who contacted us. By vendors, I mean all of those companies, such as the dot-coms, that phoned to offer various e-commerce-related products and services. If we could route all the vendor calls to one person in our organization—me—we could categorize them in a way that permitted apples-to-apples comparisons.

Why was this such a big deal? Because vendors hire very tenacious, extremely skilled sales people to work the phones. These people would get somebody's name within our company, speak with that person and see if they could interest them enough to get an appointment to visit us. If they succeeded in getting the appointment, great. If not, they would be on the phone trying to contact another person at the company—usually someone in the cubicle next to the last person contacted. What eventually ended up happening is that someone with decision-making authority would say "no" only to have the vendor show up at our doorstep because somebody else—usually an ambitious young associate trying to make a name for himself—had invited him in. Basically, the right hand didn't know what the left hand was doing. The vendors were astute enough to know that if they played the game long enough they would eventually find a weak link and get themselves in the door.

When this process is played out several hundred times a month, it's clear that a lot of chaos can result. In many instances, we weren't getting the best services at the most competitive price. Worse, we were placed in a reactive situation by having vendors tell us what we needed. Given all the hype that e-commerce companies fed us, it was a bad situation indeed.

Vendors are like cockroaches. They keep coming no matter what you try to do. Put up a trap here and they'll figure out a way around it by going there. Only one insecticide is strong enough to stop them: have all the calls go through one person or a small group of people with access to a common tracking database.

By having all the calls come through me, I could categorize the vendors and then match our needs with the exact service being offered by a particular vendor group. In this way, we'd be proactive. It was a simple plan in theory. The implementation of it would be another story.

Gerald Hogan and Maxine Lancaster supported the concept. We even got the company phone operators to direct the calls to me, in most cases. True to form, however, the folks in the U.S. division wanted to do things their own way. They took the calls themselves. This meant that the division continued to fall prey to all the games played by the vendors.

As for me, I was soon taking ten to twenty calls a day. It seemed like I spent all my time on the phone. This wasn't a bad thing, as I was able to start seeing patterns in the way vendors liked to talk. Many times, vendors would call and speak gibberish. Here's a typical example, transcribed from an actual voicemail message I received:

"Hello, my name is Jim. I work with 'Alfuh.com,' formerly 'Zatuh.com.' I wanted to touch base with you regarding e-commerce and e-business. We can provide you with perspective as regards e-business and e-commerce, as well as we have a couple B2C properties in which we run. Some of our customers are…. Umm, basically, we take a static Web site and make it more interactive. Like I say, we can give you some perspective in that regard. We also provide B2C and B2B portals for your customers. Umm, and integrating all your other areas of the company. Again, my name is Jim and my phone number is…."

Do you know what this person is offering? Neither do I. Do you think I called him back? Would you? By the way, note the "formerly Zatuh.com" mention. This dot-com has apparently changed ownership or something in its short history. Another bad sign.

Sometimes if I'm unfortunate enough to speak with a person like this live, I'll interrupt them and say, "I'm sorry, but I'm not a technical person. Would you please explain this to me in English?" Occasionally, this works. More often though, the caller is working off a script or—most likely—wants to keep it purposefully confusing so that I'll be "forced" to invite them in for a face-to-face meeting. If I think it's the first reason, I end the call. If I believe that the vendor is just trying to confuse me, I'll say to them, "Explain this to me in a single sentence, like they do in TV Guide. You know, 'Tonight on *Seinfeld*, Jerry and Elaine force George to get a job.' I want it that simple." If this doesn't work, I'll give them one last chance. "Look, explain it like you're talking to a young child," I say. If they can't, it's the end of the call.

If a concept can't be explained so that a non-technical person can understand it, it probably doesn't make sense. Even the most complex ideas can be distilled down to very simple concepts. Many times I think e-commerce vendors live on buzzwords and jargon. Apparently, their rationale is "if I can make the person I'm talking to feel incompetent and think that they 'just don't get it' but that the competition does, I'll be able to make a sale."

Unfortunately, this line of reasoning works quite well by the time the vendor finds a weak link in the organization. By having all the calls come through one person—a person who's not afraid to challenge and ask questions of the vendor—the likelihood of getting bamboozled decreases exponentially. After a year of doing this, I've heard most every story in the book. If a vendor's dishonest from the initial phone call, it only goes downhill from there.

Here's another trick of vendors cold-calling: the "Old Friends" routine. It goes something like this:

Me: "Hello?"

Vendor: "Brian, its Frank Smith. How are you?"

Now I suppose most people would probably think, "Jeez, this guy knows me, but I don't recognize the voice or the name. I don't want to be rude so I'll just play along." So they say something like, "I'm doing OK, thank you. How are you, Frank?"

Not me. Instead, I'll cut right to the chase because I don't have time.

Me: "Have we spoken before?"

If we have, then I'll pull up my notes from the database. Nine times out of ten, however, when someone, whose name I don't recognize starts a phone conversation this way, I've never talked to him before.

Vendor: "No."

Me: "Why are you calling?"

Vendor: "Uh…"

Note to vendors: You'll be doing yourself a big favor if you play it straight on the phone with me and the other people you're trying to do business with. If not, the calls tend to be short.

Here's another favorite of vendors, especially consultants, which occurred with a great deal of frequency in September through December 1999:

Vendor: "I'm calling because I have a product [or service] for your company that will revolutionize the way you conduct e-commerce. Are you interested?"

Me: "Sure, what is it?"

Vendor: "Before I tell you, so that I can tailor our product [or service] for your exact needs, why don't you tell me what your e-commerce strategy is?"

This is the "I'll show you mine if you show me yours" game. I'm always tempted to then ask the vendor, "How much money do you make?" or "What's your religion?" Why? Because the question they've just posed to me is as offensive as the two I want to ask them.

If the vendor is supposedly calling me—unsolicited—with a solution, then tell me that solution. Only a sucker is going to reveal his or her company's strategy to someone he or she's never met. The vendor thinks, I suppose, that they can't lose. If I hesitate with a response, they'll jump in and say, "you *do* have an e-commerce strategy, don't you?" On the other hand, if I tell them my strategy, they've just gotten free information from me. I don't know if they're a vendor, a competitor, a company employed by a competitor or someone else who I don't want to have that information. Regardless of who's calling, I'm not telling—no matter how small the person tries to make me feel.

Thankfully, I haven't heard the "I'll show you mine" routine in several months.

Here's one last example of something that tends to happen frequently with the cockroaches:

Vendor: "I've got a million dollar idea that will utterly transform the way you do business. No one has ever done anything like this before. In fact, it's so unique, that in order for me to tell you about it, my attorney has instructed me that I have to send you a Non-Disclosure Agreement. What's your fax number?"

As I said above, I get ten to twenty calls a day, easy. I don't have time to fill out NDAs. Oh sure, early on I filled out one or two. But I soon discovered something: Anybody who wanted an NDA or confidentiality agreement filled out had an idea that I'd heard at least two times before. To me, asking somebody during an initial phone call to sign an NDA is a sign of an unsophisticated businessperson—and there are a lot of unsophisticated business people in the New Economy.

Does this mean that I won't fill out an NDA? No. At the appropriate point in a business relationship, my company will have one of its senior personnel sign a mutual agreement on behalf of the entire organization. This only happens, however, when we're very serious about pursuing a relationship. Up to this point, I make it clear to everyone I speak with that we're engaged in non-private conversations. I tell them not to disclose confidential information. Again, this is why I don't tell people my company's e-commerce strategy.

As you can see, I spend a lot of time talking with people who really hype their offering. These people try to instill a sense of fear that I "just don't get it"—but that my competition does and I'll pay dearly if I don't say yes to the product or service being presented. Unfortunately for them, I'd dealt with their type a decade before in the film business.

CHAPTER 7
HAVE WE MET BEFORE?

Almost from the first vendor phone call, I experienced a feeling of déjà vu. The glibness. The smooth talk. The outright lies and omissions of truth. Yes, I'd seen it before in the 1980s when I worked in the entertainment industry.

I had attended a certain film school in Southern California and worked for a brief period as a videotape editor in Los Angeles. I ultimately found the people and the work quite unsatisfying. Supply and demand for talented individuals is quite lopsided and, as I mentioned before, it's difficult to make a living. As one famous producer once told me over lunch, "To succeed here, you need luck, talent and skill. Or, all of above. Or, none of the above."

Hollywood, with its promise of instant fame and riches, has always attracted a certain type of person. You may know the type. They're the non-traditional, entrepreneurial people—some might call them hucksters—who like the idea of making a lot of dough with little work. Well, these same types are also attracted to Silicon Valley and the New Economy. In fact, the same ambitious and narcissistic behaviors exhibited by those in Hollywood are seen a little farther north in Silicon Valley. The only difference is that the game—and the rewards—are several times larger in the Valley than they are in Hollywood.

I'd been thinking about the analogy between the New Economy and the entertainment industry for several months, but my epiphany didn't occur until I was on one of my many trips to the Bay Area. I had arranged to meet a former colleague, Leonard, who had recently left Frederick Gold, to pursue his dot-com dream. We met at a Thai restaurant in Palo Alto for dinner. After we finished our dessert of mango and rice, Leonard wanted to talk about a company his consulting firm was representing. He leaned back in his chair, clasped his hands behind his head and said, "here's the concept for the business…."

At this exact moment, it dawned on me that Hollywood and Silicon Valley were two sides of the same coin. In the entertainment industry, writers pitched story ideas for movies to producers, studio development people and practically anyone with money who would listen. In the New Economy, the stories have been replaced by business plans, the writers replaced by hungry entrepreneurs and the studio people by venture capitalists.

In fact, Silicon Valley is to most young people today what Los Angles was in the 1980s. It's *the place* to be to fulfill one's dreams of unimaginable riches. In the '80s, a young writer hit it big if he sold a screenplay for $250K. Today, a young entrepreneur measures his successes in the millions of dollars that he may receive in an Initial Public Offering. How times change. To many people in the Valley today, $250K probably sounds downright puny.

Why are so many young people drawn to Silicon Valley? For the same reason they are to Hollywood. It's very sexy and alluring. Bright lights, big city sort of thing. In fact, many 30-and 40-somethings who began their careers in the entertainment industry have migrated to dot-coms and the Internet in an attempt to make some "real money." The dream dies hard. Similar to Hollywood, I suspect they'll find that supply and demand are not in balance. The riches are unevenly distributed in the hands of a few, despite how the media today makes it seem as though every 20-something whiz kid is driving his or her own BMW and living in a million-dollar home.

Thankfully, I'd already gotten this type of "easy money thinking" out of my system in Hollywood. I was no longer seduced by what I saw or read. In fact, I thought I was able to look at the Internet and the so-called New Economy with a very objective eye.

I'd always wondered how my experiences in the film industry would come to serve me in Corporate America. Now I knew. I'd been through the games once and I vowed not to be suckered by the glitz and glamour a second time. Unfortunately, the same couldn't be said for others at my company.

CHAPTER 8
COMING OF AGE

There's one story that beautifully demonstrates everything I've talked about so far and much of what is to follow. It encompasses the politics of a large company, the sexiness of the Internet, the outrageous behaviors of vendors and my company's burning desire to quickly become a player in the New Economy. Best of all, the story begins just days after I had returned from the Denver Meeting, when I was being asked to implement our e-commerce strategy.

Remember that in the fall of '99, excitement about the Internet was at a fever pitch. Dot-com stocks were surging, the media was filled with ads about the Internet and day-trading was emerging as the national pastime. It was in this environment that I was invited to a Very Important Meeting.

According to Burt McDonald, the person who asked me to attend, we had a one-of-a-kind opportunity. Burt was an account representative in our U.S. division and one of his largest customers was a chain of outpatient clinics. We sold a variety of products to this chain. It turned out that the parent corporation of these clinics had recently started a new online subsidiary called "Outpatient-clinic.com." The subsidiary's mission was to create a health care Web site where people could find outpatient health information for themselves.

Because my company made products for the medical industry, Outpatient-clinic.com wanted us to "partner" with them. The theory being that we would have enormous exposure to health care consumers via the Outpatient-clinic.com Web site. If we didn't oblige, Burt said, they were already in "serious talks" with a competitor and we would lose out. Given my position, I was told, it was imperative that I attend the meeting. I agreed and was glad that someone in our U.S. division was planning to include me in a decision that involved a possible alliance. After all, my role was to evaluate potential partnerships and decide if it was something that would assist us in fulfilling our e-commerce objectives.

The meeting was held on a brutally humid September day in a room that lacked adequate air conditioning. Worse, almost 20 people were packed in a space designed to hold perhaps ten comfortably. Everyone sat elbow to elbow around a U-shaped table. There were six people representing Outpatient-clinic.com. The rest were from our U.S. division, including representatives from two brand teams, the highest ranking IT person in the division, some of his staff and Burt McDonald.

From past assignments, I knew most of the Frederick Gold people in the room. Ron Finkle, the high-ranking IT person, was someone I'd worked with in my most recent rotation. He was a very emotional person who fancied himself as being on the cutting edge of the New Economy. Ron had been at our company for almost 30 years.

The meeting would also be my first chance to meet Burt McDonald. He was reputed to do whatever it took to please his accounts. Looking at him now, I found this hard to believe. He was a small, nondescript man who was all smiles. Still, I knew he carried a big stick.

Our meeting was scheduled over the lunch hour, so we chatted informally at first as we worked through our boxed meals of processed turkey loaf. Given the tone of the conversations around the table, it was clear that many of the people from my company had previously met the representatives from Outpatient-clinic.com. This didn't surprise me, but I did note that most everyone in the room was knowledgeable about what Outpatient-clinic.com was offering us. Everyone, that is, but me.

After eating, we got down to business. Edward Torkelson, Outpatient-clinic.com's president, did most of the talking. He was a slender man with oversized glasses and a lot of nervous energy. His eyes were constantly darting around when he spoke. I struggled to focus on his words.

Edward explained that Outpatient-clinic.com wanted to have a "charter relationship" with us. He believed that the existing relationship between our company and his parent company should be expanded to include their new Internet venture. Although I understood the relationship between our two companies up to this time, I wasn't convinced that the people from Outpatient-clinic.com understood the Internet. In fact, by the time Edward finished speaking, I began to doubt whether he owned a computer.

When I expressed concern that their company didn't have experience in the online world, Edward immediately sought to allay my fears. Outpatient-clinic.com, he said, had recently struck a deal whereby they would be the "exclusive" content provider of health care information for a large, well-known Web site that many health care consumers visited. I'll call this site "Deluxe-health.com." In turn, Deluxe-health.com had only weeks before signed its own multi-million dollar deal with America Online to be the "exclusive" provider of information for AOL's general health care section.

Edward said I shouldn't be concerned with Outpatient-clinic.com's lack of Internet experience since it was aligned with Deluxe-health.com, and by association, with AOL.

The logic went something like this: 18 million people a month visit AOL and some of these people will go to the general health care section, which is "owned" by Deluxe-Health.com. Prior to Deluxe-health.com signing its deal with AOL, two million individuals each month visited the Deluxe-health site. This number "could only increase" with the AOL deal. Finally, with Outpatient-clinic.com being the "exclusive" provider of information to Deluxe-health.com's outpatient health section, we

had a great opportunity before us to get our name in front of outpa-
tients everywhere. In fact, Edward said, the "third most-visited section"
on Deluxe-health.com was outpatient health care.

In their minds, the opportunity must have looked something like
this:

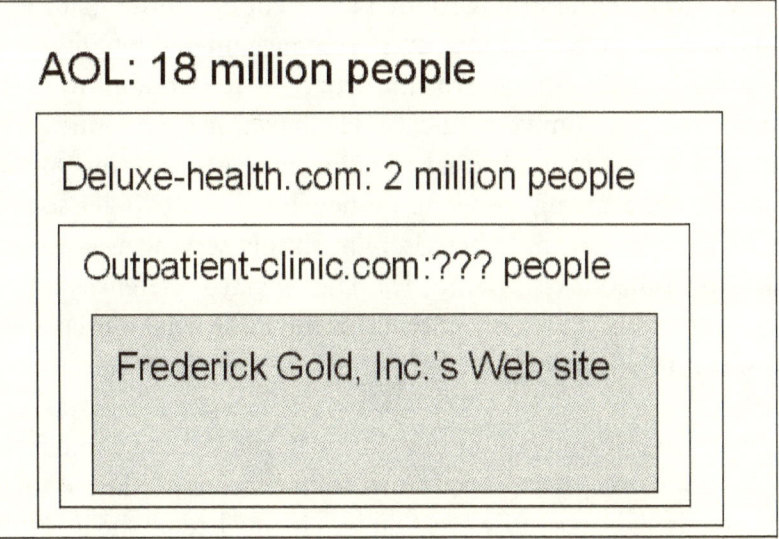

"We'll have access to all those AOL and Deluxe-health.com eyeballs,"
Edward said cheerfully, "which means that you'll have access to them, as
well. Can't you just imagine the exposure you'll get if you have a charter
relationship with us?"

I could imagine it, but I wasn't convinced of it. There was too much
here that wasn't defined. For example, what, exactly, was a "charter relationship?" I also wanted more information about what it meant for
Outpatient-clinic.com to be the "exclusive" outpatient health content
provider on Deluxe-health.com.

I recalled a conversation from my previous position when I told my
boss about a company that wanted to "partner" with us. I was very
excited. I started to tell him all the great things that would occur if we

partnered. He listened patiently until I finished. Then he said, "what exactly do they mean by 'partner'?" I didn't provide a very good answer. "It's been my experience," he said, "that when people call and say they want to partner, they actually want us to provide them with money."

I was hurt. Of course my boss was right. I'd almost been shafted.

Now, sitting in the stifling room, I knew enough to see that I was facing the same situation. Almost every sentence uttered by Edward mentioned the New Economy verb "monetize," as in "we want to monetize Outpatient-clinic.com very quickly." He may have been touting a "partnership" with us but it was clear all he really wanted was our money.

I don't mind giving someone money, but I want to get something very tangible in return. Otherwise, I'm simply serving as a no-interest banker for someone else's lame idea. The repeated references to "monetizing the venture" clued me in that this might be what our customer—who was now, in my mind, a vendor—was looking for: a zero-interest gift.

I began to ask some questions. Immediately, other people from my company starting getting impatient. "Look," I said, "I just want some more details." The response was that we already had all the information we needed. If we didn't act now, our competitor would strike first and we'd be shut out. The tension level was rising quickly.

At one point, Ron, our high-ranking IT person, leaned over to Edward and said in a pseudo-whisper loud enough for everyone in the room to hear: "He's new in his job and doesn't exactly know what he's doing. Don't worry, we'll take care of it."

It now became clear. I was the wet-behind-the-ears first-time manager who was being brought in to rubber stamp a deal that had apparently been negotiated prior to the meeting.

Well, I wasn't going to play along. The whole thing smelled fishy. At a minimum, there hadn't been any fact checking to verify what Outpatient-clinic.com was telling us. To top it off, they were hinting at a deal somewhat north of a million dollars for something of very questionable value—and something that had never been done before. I like risk, but this amounted to negligence.

I pushed forward. "I don't want to delay this. All I'm asking is that we conduct a little due diligence," I said. "Just give me two weeks to confirm the information we've been presented here today." The bottom line is that the group reluctantly gave me two weeks, "but not a day more."

A mutual non-disclosure agreement was signed and in the days ahead, I worked on a variety of issues simultaneously. The two most important were the gathering of basic data and creating a valuation model for the deal. Apparently, no one up to this point had considered how we should value such a relationship. They were just going to pay the asking price.

My model was simple. It was based upon cost-per-lead, meaning how much it would cost us for each person who eventually visited our Web site from links placed on Outpatient-clinic.com. Given what Outpatient-clinic.com had told us, this seemed like a fair way to analyze the situation. Of course, for my model to work I needed confirmation on the number of visitors to the outpatient health section of Deluxe-health.com, the section for which Outpatient-clinic.com was providing content.

As best as I could tell, there was a distribution chain being built here. It went like this: AOL-> Deluxe-health.com-> Outpatient-clinic.com-> (maybe) Ross Gold Inc.'s Web site. Everything I'd read told me that the Internet was going to simplify distribution. This was anything but simple. Given what was being proposed, my company didn't appear to be getting any closer to health care consumers. If anything, more layers were being placed between them and us.

It was getting too complicated. The whole thing appeared to be a variation on a pyramid scheme, with each player who joined later in the game footing the expenses of those who joined earlier. I wasn't convinced that a visitor to AOL would make it all the way through the different layers (at least three, by my count) to my company's Web site.

Hence, my model took into account "leakage." By this, I mean that at each step, perhaps only 30% of the people would choose to click-through and visit the next level.

As I said earlier, there was still one critical piece missing: the actual number of visitors to the outpatient health section of Deluxe-health.com, which is where the links to our Web site would appear. Edward had told us at our meeting a week earlier that this was the "third most-visited" part of Deluxe-health.com and that Deluxe-health.com was getting over two million unique visitors per month. The assumption being that "third most-visited" implied a very large number. Still, the definition was too ill-defined for me. I wanted a specific number.

For days, I kept making my request. For days, it was denied. I began to get suspicious that there was more to the story than Outpatient-clinic.com was letting on. Or worse, that they realized they'd been snookered by Deluxe-health.com and were now looking to buy themselves out of it with our money.

I was feeling pressure from others at my company who were now calling daily to check on my progress. Even though I didn't have all the information I needed, I still made my recommendation—ahead of schedule.

Based upon my findings from the last twelve days, I said that we should pursue negotiations with Outpatient-clinic.com for a pilot project. I viewed this as fairly non-committal because it enabled me to buy some more time while I waited for the additional information to surface. Since Outpatient-clinic.com had not provided me the visitor information that I needed, I used estimates from other sources to develop a working model of how a potential deal would be valued.

In hindsight, my model was quite generous. In a best-case scenario, we would be looking at paying Outpatient-clinic.com something in the mid-to-high six-figure range each year. In a worst-case scenario, the amount would be around $75,000 to $150,000. My valuation was based on measurable outcomes, which is, I believe, the only reasonable way to assess the value of a deal like this.

Three days later, Burt McDonald, the account representative for Outpatient-clinic.com, and I met to review the recommendation and discuss next steps. At that meeting, it was agreed that whatever the outcome was, the e-commerce team would handle the negotiations from this point forward. Burt would "wash his hands" of the matter.

In early October, I began discussions with Edward and Outpatient-clinic.com. Joining me were two brand team associates. It was obvious from the start that even though Outpatient-clinic.com came to us, our company was expected to spell out what it was we wanted from the deal. We obliged and gave them a list of items. We then asked them to put together a proposal, which they did by the middle of the month.

Their plan called for us to pay a whopping $7 million over a three-year period, with $3.5 million payable in year one and $1.75 million each in years two and three. The amount was outrageous. It went against everything Preacher Man had told us about start-up companies being desperate, and that we would not have to pay them anything. Indeed, this was a venture with no experience, zero revenue and nothing except good intentions and a concept. For comparison, we could have acquired a substantial equity interest in numerous dot-coms for this amount. There was no equity involved here. I still don't know how anyone could have possibly come up with a valuation this high. The proposal caused us to have serious doubts about Outpatient-clinic.com and Edward.

When we spoke after the proposal was received, Edward asked me, "Is this amount in the ballpark of what you were expecting?" My response: "It's not even in the same city where the ballpark's located."

Around this time, the information we'd requested about the "exclusive" relationship with Deluxe-health.com made its way to us. Suffice it to say that the relationship was not exclusive—as defined in the dictionary. Our conversations with representatives of Deluxe-health revealed that they would continue to get outpatient health care information from other sources, *in addition to* Outpatient-clinic.com.

Most disturbing of all was when we were finally told the actual number of Deluxe-health visitors who made it to the outpatient health care section of the site. It was this section which had the content provided "exclusively" by Outpatient-clinic.com. Recall that Outpatient-clinic.com had told us for weeks that this section was the "third most-visited" portion on Deluxe-health.com, but was unable to provide actual numbers. As it turned out, of the approximately 2.4 million unique visitors to Deluxe-health.com's home page each month, only about 35,000—less than 2% of the total number of unique visitors—actually made it to the section where Outpatient-clinic.com was providing information.

A revised graphic—to scale—of what Outpatient-clinic.com was proposing looked like this:

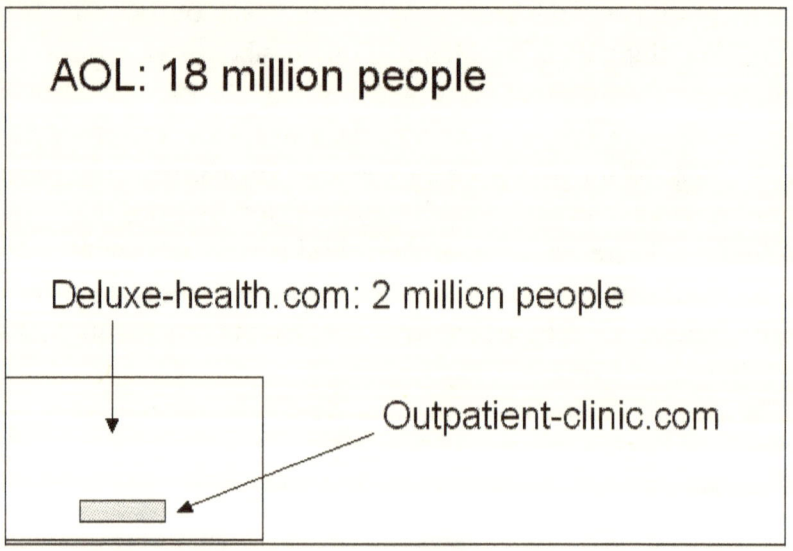

The Outpatient-clinic.com box represented the "opportunity" that they were presenting to us.

The visitor numbers justified my valuation model's extreme worst-case scenario. We were looking at perhaps something in the low six figures and most likely something in the five-figure range on an annual basis for the deal. I told Edward this and he said, "No problem, a hundred grand is fine."

At this point, Edward lost all credibility. This was clearly a grab for money. Consider an analogous situation. Say I'm a homebuyer and I come to you as the seller and ask what the price of your house is. You tell me $7 million. I say, "that's too rich for my blood, I've only got $100 thousand to spend." You then say, "Fine. Sold for $100 thousand." Of course I'd be just a little suspect of what I was getting for you to drop the price that much immediately.

Since a picture's worth a thousand words, here's how Edward's valuation of the deal, drawn to scale, now appeared:

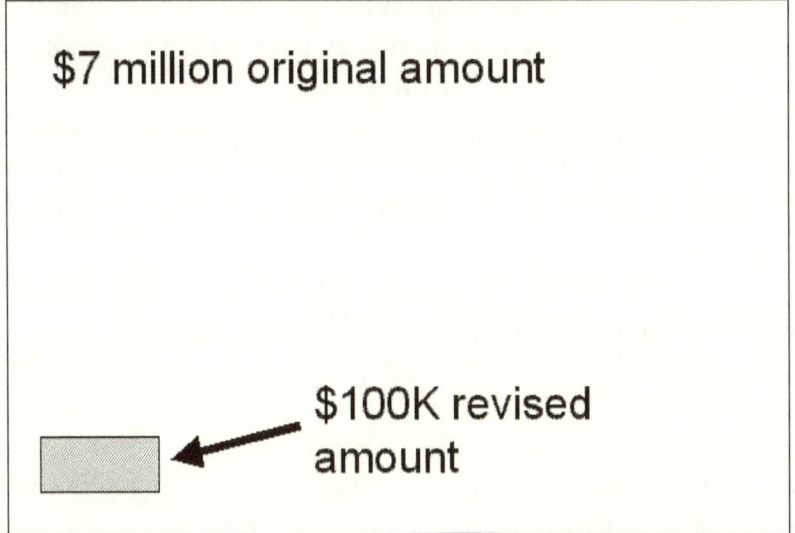

Over the next few days, a couple of strange things happened. First, Edward was suddenly—and without explanation—replaced by another person, Monique Zucker, from the parent company of Outpatient-clinic.com. Monique, as I understood it, negotiated the parent company's contracts for the products we sold to their outpatient clinics. Monique admitted during our first phone call that the $7 million proposed amount was "stupid." Next, when asked to comment about Deluxe-health.com's site traffic, there was no response for a week. Near the end of October, I was told that the relationship with Deluxe-Health was not important. Instead, Monique suggested that the proper way to value the deal was to focus on the "crossover" of health care consumers who would visit Outpatient-clinic.com instead of physically coming to the outpatient clinics. I didn't understand this new business model.

By now, things had become even more confusing. After looking at all the events over the past several weeks, we began to question what we had been told. I decided that now was an opportune time to step back from the situation and let Outpatient-clinic.com regroup.

On November 1, after discussing the situation with my two associates, I sent an e-mail to Monique stating that we were evaluating a number of options. I said we would get back to them in the next couple of weeks with specific ideas in response to their $7 million proposal.

Apparently, this message did not sit well with Monique, who immediately contacted Burt McDonald, and, from what I can tell, expressed outrage at the way she'd been treated. She felt we were stringing them along. I saw it as protecting our interests.

Over the next several days, while I was out of the office attending a conference, I understand that the CEO of Outpatient-clinic.com's parent company demanded to see high-ranking people at Frederick Gold. His request was initially denied. I then learned via a forwarded voice-mail message that the CEO and Monique had gotten their wish granted. They would fly their corporate jet in for a little meeting with Burt, the two associates and me.

As promised, Monique and the CEO did come to our offices. Arnie Uffleman was dressed like a typical new-money CEO, with his enormous Rolex and oversized gold cufflinks. After exchanging pleasantries, Arnie began the discussion by saying, "Gentlemen, let me take a minute to tell you about the right way to conduct negotiations." Apparently, in Arnie's mind, there was only one "right way" to negotiate. For the next fifteen minutes, we were subjected to The World According to Arnie. He'd built his business from the ground up, he said. Although he wanted us to participate in his dream, he certainly understood if we chose not to. He then dropped a not-so-subtle reminder that his outpatient clinics bought a lot of product from our company. After he finished his monologue, we discussed our disagreements and resolved to contact them in two weeks with a go/no-go decision—essentially what I had proposed in my e-mail a week earlier.

Two comments by Arnie stood out. First, that Outpatient-clinic.com was going to focus on a "business-to-business" model. This was distinctly different from the consumer-focused model they had been pitching for the last several weeks. Second, he said the venture was highly speculative and might not pan out. I informed them that we were looking to make investments, not speculate, given our budget and mandate in the e-commerce group.

The next day, I received a call from Monique. She was livid. For 15 minutes, she went off on a tirade about the way we were treating her and Outpatient-clinic.com. Arnie, I was told, was too much of a gentleman to say the things that Monique was now telling me, but she wanted to make sure that I heard them. At one point near the end of her outburst, Monique echoed what Arnie had said about her firm spending a lot of money with us. She then said, "you're going to end our relationship with your company."

That didn't sit well with me. I'd thought that the meeting with her and Arnie was a not-so-subtle attempt at extortion. If we didn't support their dot-com start-up, they wouldn't buy product from us for their outpatient clinics. Now she was confirming my suspicion. The game was over.

I interrupted her. "Monique, I don't respond well to this type of pressure. Based on what you're telling me, I think it's best if we terminate our discussions at this point. Your company and mine have been talking for several weeks and I still don't understand exactly what the value is for us. However, I clearly understand what the value is between us and your company concerning our existing relationship, which I want you to know we greatly appreciate. It's just that I'm not sure exactly what the vision is for Outpatient-clinic.com."

"Are you saying that you don't want to continue negotiations?"

"That's what I'm saying."

"Do what you want," she said and then hung up.

I immediately sent a voicemail message to Burt McDonald and the others who had been involved in the negotiations to let them know that we were finished talking with Outpatient-clinic.com.

That evening, I slept the best I had in weeks. For the first time in my career, I'd actually made a significant business decision on my own. No committees. No endless meetings. Just me knowing that I did something in the best interest of my company and its shareholders. I felt wonderful. We had avoided parting with $7 million on a questionable venture.

Unfortunately, the story doesn't end here. The next morning, I got a call from an outraged Burt McDonald. He was even angrier than Monique had been a day earlier. Before I knew it, several executive-level people at Frederick Gold were being called. I apparently had just teed off a very important customer and was about to lose the company millions of dollars because of my supposed stupidity.

In rapid order, a meeting was arranged at Russell Dunn's office with Maxine Lancaster, Gerald Hogan, Burt and several senior people from our U.S. division. There was only one name conspicuously omitted from the list of invitees. Mine. I viewed it as a trial in absentia. My decision was to be reviewed, but I wouldn't be allowed to defend myself.

Shortly before the meeting took place, Gerald and Maxine invited me to come. I asked if they felt I had conducted myself appropriately during the negotiations. They said yes. In fact, they were quite pleased with my work to date and the manner in which I had handled the Outpatient-clinic.com decision. I thanked them for the invite, but respectfully declined the offer. Instead, I asked them to convey their confidence in me to the other attendees.

From what I understand, the group supported my decision but agreed that it could have perhaps been handled in a better manner. I accept that. They also noted that Burt could have done a better job of telling me what had transpired between him and Outpatient-clinic.com prior to my being brought into the picture. In this way, Burt could have saved face in front of his customer.

For several days after The Review, I thought the event would have a chilling effect on the way I conducted myself. For a time, it did. I believe a lot of people at large corporations get timid and avoid taking sensible risk if they think their decisions may negatively impact their career. It's easier to keep a low profile and avoid conflict. I understand this. And to some extent, I keep a lower profile today than I did a year ago.

At this point, you may be wondering what ever happened with Outpatient-clinic.com. The last I heard, the U.S. division had tossed them a bone of $50,000 to do some Internet work. Many months later, Outpatient-clinic.com still hadn't delivered. I doubt they ever will. By the way, in spite of Outpatient-clinic.com's sword-rattling that I was going to doom the relationship between our two companies, we still do business with them. Of course, they're now upset about another issue completely unrelated to our aborted project and are once again threatening to stop buying our products.

And what of Deluxe-health.com? As with Outpatient-clinic.com, the caffeine is wearing off—quickly. They're burning through cash so fast, the folks on Wall Street doubt they'll last through the end of the year. Interestingly, they called me recently to discuss another deal. They were so desperate for cash that they offered to fly their CEO down to speak with me in person. Well, given my experience above, my days of talking with flying CEOs is over. I sent them the following e-mail message:

"At this time, given the market's uncertainty surrounding your enterprise, we believe that it is in the best interest of our shareholders to wait until the viability of Deluxe-health.com as an ongoing concern is clarified. Please feel free to contact me in three months."

You'd think this would be the end of it. It wasn't. Hope springs eternal at dot-coms and they still weren't hearing the Fat Lady sing. I received the following e-mail message within minutes:

"I respect your position, however, as I beleive [sic] events will soon change in our favor, I would like to be able to forward you information that speaks to the accomplishments that are incurring [sic] here on a regular basis. The proposals that we are submitting are done in a way as to minimize the risk to the client (i.e., performance based contracts, payment in arears [sic]). So, I will continue to keep you informed. Thanks."

What about my relationship with Burt McDonald, our Outpatient-clinic.com account representative? Burt was moved to another position. He and I still talk with one another, but not about this particular topic.

Ron Finkle, the person who publicly humiliated me during the initial meeting with Outpatient-clinic.com, used the situation to his political advantage. For months, he had wanted to be more involved in e-commerce strategy for the company. However, as an IT person, he always felt left out of key decisions made by the marketing group. Knowing that the U.S. division's president still wanted his own Internet Center of Excellence, Ron started drawing up plans to create such a group, to be called the "e-business team." It would duplicate our Global e-Commerce group, except that it was housed in the U.S. division—not corporate. More importantly, Ron made sure that he led the team, a position that would take him from the IT function into a marketing role. Better still, he would report directly to the president of the U.S. division. Ten months later, his dream became a reality: A second, and some believed, redundant group at Frederick Gold was established to handle e-commerce issues.

In sum, Outpatient-clinic.com was my first Big Test. It was a coming of age for me. Yes, it was a painful experience, but it prepared me well for the other ordeals that were yet to come.

When I tell people the Outpatient-clinic.com story, they inevitably ask if I would still do what I did knowing what the possible consequences were. Without hesitation, I tell them I would.

CHAPTER 9
THE 800-POUND GORILLA

A couple weeks after the Outpatient-clinic.com fiasco, we had our first-ever group staff meeting. Actually, it was a meeting that consisted of the e-commerce team and a couple of other groups that reported to Maxine Lancaster. It was your typical staff meeting, with the exception that it was being held at a remote wooded retreat outside of town.

At one point, Maxine got up to take a phone call in one of the side rooms. A couple minutes later, she emerged and motioned for me to join her.

As I made my way around the table where my colleagues sat, I felt a mix of embarrassment and pride; embarrassment that I was disrupting the meeting and pride that Maxine was asking me into the other room. I'd learned from past experiences that when this happened she wanted my advice on some potential opportunity that had come our way. I was hoping this would be the case now.

When I entered the room, Maxine was sitting on a couch, looking at me with a Cheshire cat-like smile.

"Your 'friends' called," she said cryptically.

"What friends might those be?"

"The ones at 'Hypemeister.com.' You remember them, don't you?"

How could I forget? This was a company that fancied itself the 800-pound gorilla for our industry on the Internet. Every newspaper reporter in the country got a quote from someone at this company or mentioned them in their article whenever they wrote about the medical products industry.

I had visited with some executives of Hypemeister.com several months before. In fact, the trip occurred two months prior to my promotion. Hypemeister had invited us to their corporate offices in Minneapolis to discuss a possible "partnership." I was asked to attend because I'd done some research on the company. In fact, of the people who went to the meeting from Frederick Gold, Inc., I was the most knowledgeable about Hypemeister.

From what I could tell, they were masters at working the media and spinning lots of PR. Aside from that, I didn't see very much to the company. After meeting with them, I was even more convinced. In fact, one writer later labeled them a "shell company." I concur.

Our meeting came at a time when they were literally in the papers every day. They were working off hype like it was going out of style. It was clear that the people employed by the company—from the highest levels on down—were carpet-baggers from Silicon Valley and elsewhere who thought they could make an easy buck by cleaning up the "waste and redundancy" in the health care industry. It made for very appealing headlines. The only problem was, they didn't have any industry experience or any credibility except what they got the newspapers to generate. Hence, they needed an industry partner in the worst way. So we were invited to visit.

They'd previously come to our offices and presented their pitch to our senior leadership team. They had also called on all of our competitors. No one was interested in partnering. Now we were visiting with them on their turf in Minneapolis. At this meeting, we were to learn exactly what they meant by "partnership" and how much money they wanted to charge us for the privilege.

A striking young blonde woman with a charming Irish accent gave most of their presentation. Like many men in the New Economy, she was an engaging speaker, but she didn't say much of substance. It was just a lot of fluff. In hindsight, this is quite typical of Internet companies. Sell the sizzle. Forget the facts—they only get in the way.

Finally, the moment of truth arrived. We asked how much money they wanted. "For a charter sponsorship with Hypemeister.com," Ms. Ireland announced proudly, "the membership cost is $100 million for four years."

There was complete silence in the room. Those of us in attendance from my company, including Maxine Lancaster and myself, said nothing. It took everything I had not to burst out laughing. $100 million was—is—a ridiculously large amount of money for what they were offering, which was essentially the ability for us to run banner ads on their Web site.

One of our team members asked the Hypemeister.com folks if they would leave the room for a moment so we could discuss the matter in private. They obliged. When the last Hypemeister.com person was out the door, all of us starting laughing. I wasn't the only one who thought the $100 million amount was ludicrous. My colleagues just had better poker faces than I. Once the peals of laughter subsided, we agreed that the sum was too much and that we didn't think the company had much to offer. However, we wanted to stay in touch with them on the off chance that they got traction in the marketplace.

We called the Hypemeister people back into the room and shared our thoughts with them. As we were parting ways, their young CEO eagerly went around shaking everybody's hand—everybody, that is, who was at a director level and above. As the only associate-level person in the room, this meant that he didn't shake my hand. Too bad. Of all the people my company brought on that trip, there was only one of us who had deep-level knowledge of Hypemeister. Me. It would be an unfortunate faux pax. On the plane ride home, we were still laughing about the arrogance of the CEO and his minions.

That was six months ago. I thought we'd heard the last of Hypemeister.com. I thought wrong.

Maxine Lancaster had now stopped grinning at me. I took a seat across from her.

"Why did they call?"

"We're going to do a deal with them."

I was too stunned to say anything.

"They called Fred Silver and offered to buy Zypher Corporation from us. In exchange for their purchase of Zypher at a preferential price, we'll agree to spend $50 million over two years to sponsor certain portions of their Web site."

This was a lot to take in. Fred Silver was our CFO and no slouch when it came to the numbers. Zypher was a company we had purchased a few years before that turned out to be a dog. We'd basically written it off the books. The $50 million, however, was the strangest part of all.

"Maxine, didn't Hypemeister want $100 million from us over a four-year period when we visited with them a few months ago? It sure seems like $50 million over two years is the equivalent of $100 million over four years."

"It is."

"So why are we doing this? Didn't we agree that the deal stunk?"

"We did, but Fred wants to do it and that's that."

"So Fred's been negotiating with them and we weren't involved? Fred didn't even go on the trip to their offices last July."

Maxine explained that Fred was desperate to dump Zypher. It was a drain on our resources.

"If that's the case, then why is Hypemeister so anxious to get it?"

"They couldn't care less about the company. Hypemeister just wants the doctors associated with Zypher so they can convert them over to their product. This is part of their attempt to build critical mass for their Web site. They're betting that by getting enough customers, they'll become the industry standard."

That part made sense, but I still didn't understand why we had to spend money to sponsor their Web site.

"Couldn't we just sell them Zypher and leave it at that?"

"You weren't listening. I said they'll pay us a better price if we agree to sponsor them."

"It would have to be a hell of a better price."

"It is."

"Are they paying us in cash?"

Maxine hesitated. "Fred says the deal is they'll pay us in stock."

"What? That stock is incredibly volatile. It's been as high as $140 and as low as $15 in the last six months. I think it's trading around $50 currently. Isn't Fred concerned about it dipping again?"

"He is, which is why he's working to get price protection in the form of a collar to prevent downside risk."

Maxine meant that Fred had made a request to have a limit—a "collar"—placed on the deal so that if Hypemeister's stock price dipped below, say $40, the deal would be terminated or we would receive additional shares to make us receive the equivalent value of $50 per share.

"I still don't like it."

"Our job is simply to tell Fred what we want from Hypemeister regarding sponsorship. We want to get beyond banner ads and make sure we're getting something of measurable value for our money. Do you have your computer with you?"

"Yes."

"Bring it in here and start working on the deal. Hypemeister is sending down its negotiating team tomorrow morning. We need to get to terms in 48 hours. Better call Dan and Luke."

I went back out to the staff meeting and retrieved my computer, all the while averting my gaze from the stares of my colleagues. Maxine went out to rejoin her meeting.

While the computer was firing up, I used the phone to call Dan and Luke. Dan "The Man" Bosley was our attorney. An ex-marathoner, he was a very competitive person. He was also the most knowledgeable lawyer at my company when it came to IT and Internet issues. To top it off, he knew how to draw up a mean contract.

Luke Stone was his partner in crime. A financial whiz from our Corporate Finance group, he was the most laid back Harvard MBA I'd ever known. A big man, he was slow speaking, but quite smart; he never made others feel as though they were lacking ability. Both men had been part of the group that met with Hypemeister several months ago.

Working as a team, Dan-the-Man, Luke and I spent the afternoon drafting documents and e-mailing them back and forth. By day's end, we managed to create a plan for our negotiating strategy. Given the circumstances, we felt relatively prepared for what lay ahead. Beginning at 10 a.m. sharp tomorrow, we would all participate in the negotiations with Hypemeister. Maxine Lancaster would also be joining us and serving as the lead negotiator.

The next morning, the Hypemeister folks arrived right on schedule. We ushered them up to a conference room and began the meeting. Their lead negotiator was a young hotshot from UC-Berkeley. His name was Nathan Dirk. Clean-cut and innocent in appearance, he made sure that he placed himself at the head of the table when they came into the room.

The negotiations were tedious. Neither side really wanted to close the deal that had been agreed to by the executives. Nathan kept saying, "Look, I don't want to get involved in a shot-gun marriage. If this isn't going to work, let's just walk away." I wanted to take him up on his offer. Unfortunately, given the agreement-in-principle reached by Fred Silver, we couldn't.

One point of contention was how we would measure performance. They wanted the measurement to be the number of "impressions" that our banner ads received. Impressions being the number of times a banner ad appears on a Web site—whether or not the visitor actually sees the ad and clicks on it.

We thought this was a bogus standard. Instead, we asked to value the sponsorship based upon the amount of time visitors spent on the portion of the Web site we would sponsor. This couldn't possibly be done, they informed us. It was the industry standard to measure based upon impressions.

"You fancy yourself the industry leader, don't you?" Maxine asked.

"Yes," they replied.

"Well, here's an opportunity for you to show leadership and redefine how to measure success."

After much discussion, it was decided that we would meet periodically with Hypemeister.com during the contract's first year to redefine measurements for the second year. It was a meaningless compromise.

We continued to work through other issues large and small. Even though the terms were slightly less onerous to us, I still felt that the deal didn't make any sense. Worse, it was becoming clear that I would be the person primarily responsible for implementing the deal. Although I understood the rationale of having someone who actively participated in the negotiations also be involved in the implementation, I didn't want the assignment. Knowing what I did about Hypemeister.com, I knew implementing the agreement was going to be a difficult endeavor.

That evening, we had dinner delivered and then worked late into the night. Nothing definitive was decided during this first day of negotiations.

Day Two got off to a bad start. As Dan-the-Man, Luke and I worked through a problem, we inadvertently left Nathan Dirk and the Hypemeister attorney sitting in our lobby for over an hour. When we realized this, I went down and brought them upstairs. As I opened the door to our conference room, I was overcome by a powerful stench. The cold cuts and cole slaw that we had catered in the day before had been left sitting out over night. I took away the food, but we couldn't get rid of the smell.

I went to find Dan-the-Man and Luke to resume our negotiations. Today it would just be the three of us and the two Hypemeister folks. Regrettably, it took me another 45 minutes to track down my colleagues. When we returned to the conference room, Nathan and his attorney were steaming.

"I just don't understand," Nathan moaned. "First you make us wait in the lobby for an hour-and-a-half. Then you bring us into this room that smells like crap. And if that weren't enough punishment, you keep us waiting for another 45 minutes." He shook his head slowly. There were tears of anger in his eyes.

On that note, our second day of negotiations began. It was slow going but we did make some progress. The payment schedule and terms were ones we could live with and most of the details were fair. All that needed to be done was the actual drafting of the contract. This is a tedious back-and-forth process that involves the attorneys arguing about pretty much every single word.

By the time we reached the contracting stage, we had passed the 48-hour deadline set by Fred Silver, but we still persevered. It was now approaching 9 p.m. I had a date scheduled for that evening and I didn't want to miss it—especially given the vow I'd made during the meeting in Denver to maintain a life outside of work. Dan-the-Man and Luke were upset that I was "walking out" at this point. But I would have added very little value to the process.

The next morning, I found a copy of the contract in my e-mail. The time stamp was 4 a.m. Dan-the-Man and Luke definitely earned their pay the day (and night) before. Aside from some changes here and there, the contract was final and we signed it—less than 72 hours from the time Maxine Lancaster pulled me out of the staff meeting to tell me that we'd be negotiating a deal with Hypemeister.

Who says an Old Economy company can't move at Internet Speed?

In hindsight, the contracting process seemed like child's play compared to the implementation of the deal.

As I had suspected, I was put in charge of overseeing the agreement. It was a task that I dreaded. I had a deep mistrust of the people at Hypemeister.com. As I said, I thought they were carpet-baggers out for a quick buck.

At our first face-to-face implementation meeting, the Hypemeister folks were visibly surprised to learn that I was leading the implementation. I suppose they were eager to spin their hype on some other rube in our company.

They may have had the media's attention, but they didn't have any real knowledge about how our industry worked. It was their hope and dream that we would just willingly share with them our expertise gained from over 100 years of operations. There was no way that was going to happen.

The one thing I remember from this first meeting is Ms. Ireland asking me how I would define success for our relationship. I reiterated what we told them during our meeting six months prior: "Success means we increase market share for our products in a measurable way." It was pretty simple.

I then asked her how she would define success. The question appeared to catch her completely off guard. Apparently, she had never thought about this from her company's perspective. She had our money—which was enough to cover their payroll expenses for at least the next two years—and that was all she was concerned about. Ms. Ireland had always been quite smooth when she was presenting. I'd never seen her lose her composure like this. "Umm," she stammered, "I'd define success as speedy implementation."

"Speedy implementation?" Good God! This was going to be worse than I thought. Here was my counterpart on a $50 million deal and she didn't have a clue. To make matters worse, Ms. Ireland was probably a millionaire, given her stock options in Hypemeister. My anger level was starting to rise. This was among the biggest deals to date ever between a large company and a dot-com. And here the person sitting across from me is defining success as "speedy implementation." If the analysts from Wall Street had been sitting with us that day, Hypemeister.com stock would have crashed to a new low. It was clear that there was nothing but sizzle here.

Over the coming weeks, a parade of Hypemeister employees came through our offices. Each wanted to know our brand strategies and industry knowledge. We didn't give it to them. It wasn't necessary for them to execute the deal.

Meanwhile, Hypemeister continued its acquisition spree. Their stock was holding its own, so they figured now would be a good time to buy as much as they could before the Market figured out there was nothing behind the curtain. One of the bizarre side effects of Hypemeister's merger and acquisition activity was that during our meetings, not only would we exchange business cards with them, *they* would exchange business cards among themselves. Why? It was the first time many of the people from the newly acquired companies had met.

The acquisitions kept coming and Wall Street loved every minute of it. As a result, the stock price was nearly double what it was when we signed the deal. This was a good thing. Fred Silver, our CFO, was not able to get the price protection he had sought from Hypemeister. He took a risk that their stock would not decline in value between the time that the deal was signed and the time when we would take possession of the shares—a period of roughly ten weeks.

As it turned out, Fred gambled and won. A week before the deal closed and we received the shares, Hypemeister announced a very big acquisition that sent their stock price to the highest level it had been in months. It stayed at this level when we took possession of our shares and also when we exercised them over the coming two weeks.

We sold our shares—a large amount—in a judicious manner, to not drive down Hypemeister's market capitalization. There probably are other companies that, if they had been in our position, would have just put all their shares on the market at one time, which almost certainly would have caused Hypemeister's stock price to plummet. However, we gave Hypemeister our word that we would not jeopardize their valuation and we honored our promise.

Speaking of keeping one's word, Hypemeister had a problem with that. We were careful to insert a paragraph into the contract stating that if anything disparaging to one of our products appeared on a part of the Hypemeister.com site that we were sponsoring, we had the right to have it removed. It wasn't too long after the sponsorship began that we had the opportunity to exercise this clause.

A research physician wrote a book that made some dubious accusations about one of our products. Hypemeister, despite all its self-promoting hype that it was a source of "credible and balanced information," reprinted parts of the publication and even invited the author to an online chat. Strangely, the folks at Hypemeister never spoke with us to get our view on the matter. Other legitimate sources, including the *New York Times*, did, and realized the accusations were completely unfounded. Hypemeister eventually removed the stories from their site at our request, but never did present a retraction or clarification.

So, was the deal a success? From a financial perspective, it was. We made millions of dollars due to Hypemeister's stock appreciation *and* sold off Zypher Corporation, a non-productive asset.

But did the deal benefit us from a marketing perspective? To date, it hasn't. There have been myriad implementation problems caused by Hypemeister. In fact, the average visitor to their site would be hard-pressed to discern whether Frederick Gold, Inc. is a sponsor.

To compound matters, Wall Street finally caught on that Hypemeister.com actually needed to do something—like produce revenues—and not just acquire other companies. As a result, its stock has been hovering at a 52-week low for some time. Thankfully this depression in their stock price occurred about two weeks after we sold our last shares. Again, it points out the dumb luck that we had. Instead of coming out millions ahead, we could have easily been holding another non-productive asset (Hypemeister.com) *and* paying it $50 million over the next two years.

What of Nathan Dirk, Hypemeister's lead negotiator? The last I heard, he had left them and was working for another start-up in Silicon Valley. Say what you want about Nathan, but he knows when the caffeine's about to wear off.

Ms. Ireland, you ask? I think she's still with Hypemeister, although she's had a large turnover in her staff. I really haven't had much contact with her. For political reasons, responsibility for implementation of the deal shifted to Ron Finkle's e-business group in our U.S. division. I'm not disappointed. Someone else can have the headache.

Today, Hypemeister.com doesn't get nearly as much media attention as it did a year ago. The company is now trying to focus on living up to its hype. This won't be easy. It's been nearly a year since the contract was signed and they still aren't close to their one measure of success, "speedy implementation."

CHAPTER 10
VAPOR

Shortly after the Hypemeister negotiations, a company that I'll call "Vaporcon" came to visit. Like most New Economy firms, they sent two representatives—a man and a woman. As usual, the man, J.J., was nattily attired and feigned instant rapport. The woman, Becky, was attractive and flirtatious. Both were from the East Coast and had distinctively New Yawk accents. What impressed me most was that the sunless November weather apparently had no ill effect on their tans.

J.J. and Becky met with Maxine and me. They were selling an application that would enable doctors to communicate with patients via the Internet. Instead of using the phone or trudging to the doctor's office, people could now go online to schedule visits, view test results and complete other routine tasks.

It was an interesting concept, but we struggled to see why we were needed. After all, as it was currently designed, the application didn't help us sell any of our products or improve our relationship with either doctors or their patients.

"We're very flexible on this," J.J. said at our first meeting. "The application is about 80% built, but we can easily add additional functionality that would be of direct benefit to you. Surely there is something that would be of interest."

J.J. was smooth. Most likely, he was coming to us because the venture capital firms had heard the idea and turned him down. Still, in order to get the equivalent of zero-interest financing, he was willing to tailor his offering so there'd be something—anything—that would get us to bite. Because the e-Commerce group was under a mandate to establish alliances, we thought there might be an opportunity here. Perhaps we could design some add-on function that would provide a three-way benefit—to us, physicians, and, of course, their patients. Certainly there was some risk, but it seemed like a sensible risk to take.

As we spoke, J.J. gave us a little more to chew on. He envisioned a six-month pilot program of 500 physicians spread around the country. If successful, we could expand it to a much larger level, though it was unclear exactly how we would do this.

To sweeten the offer even further, J.J. told us the whole system would flow over broadband telecommunications lines. Although the application didn't need the high-speed lines to work, he said, having DSL or cable modems in our customers' workplaces would be an extra whiz-bang selling point. The high-speed lines didn't matter to us. We were more concerned with finding an add-on to the application that would benefit our customers and our company.

During the next few weeks, we spoke frequently with J.J. to hammer out what the final application would look like. Becky said little during our meetings and phone calls. She really served more as an observer, smiling when needed and typing notes into her laptop computer. I wasn't sure if she even understood what was going on.

At perhaps our third meeting together, Maxine hit upon an idea for the add-on application. Her concept addressed a serious problem in our industry: health care consumers' incorrect use of our products. Maxine's idea was to create an interactive online educational program. With such a program, people could get immediate answers and instruction on the correct use of our products right when they needed it. There would be no more wasted time on the phone trying to call the doctor or us.

Maxine came up with the idea by working through a schematic known as the "Transaction Tool." This was a proprietary model developed by our company. We used it to explain the different parts of the value chain in our industry. We rarely shared it with people outside the firm. Maxine, however, had shown it to Becky and J.J. so they would better understand how her proposed add-on application would enhance the offering. Becky, as usual, took copious notes.

J.J. agreed to the online educational program and our first major hurdle was behind us.

Next, we asked to see a demo of the application as it existed. So far, all we had been shown were PowerPoint slides. The Vaporcon people asked for our indulgence. Might we allow them to put the "finishing touches" on the application and add our portion before unveiling it to us? We were assured this would only take a brief period. We agreed and did not press the issue.

Up to this point, I was only tangentially involved in the project. J.J. and Becky had approached Maxine initially and she had been the one speaking with them. Now, Gerald Hogan and I were brought in to work through the details. This wouldn't have been a problem if we weren't burdened with other responsibilities. At this same time, however, we were gearing up our European e-commerce operations. Gerald and I were scheduled to attend a three-day meeting with our EU colleagues in Geneva. Coincidentally, Maxine would also be in Geneva attending a different set of meetings.

Because Maxine wanted to move quickly with Vaporcon, a transatlantic conference call was hastily arranged. The main objective for the call was to reach an agreement-in-principle on the deal terms. So it was that on our first night in Europe, Gerald, Maxine and I met in my hotel room and dialed in at the appointed hour.

Early in the call, Gerald, who was approaching the deal with fresh eyes, brought up an interesting concern. To him, it appeared as though we were providing the funding and building the *entire* application—not just our add-on portion—from scratch. He said it was analogous to us building an entire TV studio when all our company should be doing was paying to produce a single TV show.

J.J. vehemently denied this. "The application is 80% built," he told us. "You are not building a TV studio."

J.J. said this with a lot of conviction, but there was still something about his level of defensiveness that didn't ring true.

As J.J. and Gerald battled back and forth, I glanced over at Maxine. Her eyes were closed and she was breathing deeply. If I hadn't known better, I'd have said she was asleep. But I did know better. Maxine often appeared to be sleeping during meetings, when she was actually listening quite intently—with her eyes closed. I figured she wanted to test Gerald's ability to handle a negotiation.

Sure enough, the minute the call ended, Maxine opened her eyes, stood up and said, "Guys, I think we're there." It was the first of several occasions that I heard Maxine say this. What she meant was that, as far as she was concerned, the deal was done. She would be stepping out of the picture. Of course, the deal was really not completed. It would be left to somebody to do all the grunt work of actually negotiating the contract.

I was that somebody.

Now that I was responsible for hacking out the details, I started to scrutinize all of the material Vaporcon had provided. There were scores of unanswered questions. These would need to be addressed during the negotiations, which were to drag out for nearly a month.

Dan-the-Man joined me for the negotiations. Also participating was Samuel Johnson, from our contracting department, and a second attorney, Jodi McAdams.

I've never met a finer negotiator than Samuel. He knew where the fluff was and worked diligently to remove it. I want him with me when I buy my next car. As for Jodi, she didn't fit your typical profile of a corporate attorney. She looked like a fashion model and was incredibly fun-loving. Beware, however, if she thought you were taking advantage of her or the situation. She would unleash a fireball of verbal destruction that would embarrass a professional wrestler.

J.J. and Becky turned out to be the only people representing Vaporcon in the negotiations. I wondered why they didn't bring along an attorney or someone with contracting expertise. To this day, I have never had this question answered.

When Samuel, Jodi and Dan-the-Man started hearing the Vaporcon pitch for the first time, they were astounded. "There's nothing here," Dan-the-Man told me. He didn't just mean this figuratively. It was his opinion that there was no application. I told him they had confirmed for us repeatedly that there was an application and that it was 80% built. Dan-the-Man remained incredulous. "If that's the case, then they should show us something more than PowerPoint slides."

In my heart, I knew he was right, but it didn't stop me from pushing him to do the deal. "Look, I don't like it either, but Maxine Lancaster wants us to take a little risk and get a deal completed, so that's what we're going to do." Dan-the-Man said nothing.

The best we could do was pepper Vaporcon with "what-if" questions in the hopes of getting them to flesh out the concept. We asked what they would do if there were four physicians at a particular clinic but we were only interested in three of them for the pilot. Would Vaporcon provide the application to the fourth doctor? Also, what if they couldn't get the DSL installed? Would they use dial-up lines instead?

The answer to these questions and others was "we'll cross that bridge when we come to it." This wasn't exactly a comforting thought.

Two weeks into the negotiations, Becky told us that the Vaporcon CEO wanted to speak with Gerald, Maxine and me about an important matter. We quickly rearranged our calendars and arrived at work early for a 7 a.m. conference call.

After exchanging pleasantries, the head of Vaporcon told us that his company had just been purchased. "But don't worry," the CEO added quickly, "the acquiring company supports our project. The deal will go forward." He went on to say that a representative from the new company, Frankie Zee, would be joining us occasionally during our negotiations. Frankie's job was to ensure that the deal was kept on track.

The news was a shock. We took Vaporcon at their word that the acquisition would not disrupt the deal and continued to negotiate. Dan-the-Man immediately amended the contract draft to include a "change of ownership" clause.

At our next face-to-face meeting with Vaporcon, Frankie Zee made his first appearance. He was the quintessential fair-haired fraternity guy, dressed in his preppy blue blazer and striped tie. A negotiator he was not. For starters, Frankie despised details. Whenever we voiced an objection that he couldn't (or wouldn't) answer, his standard reply was "we'll work through that later."

To compound matters, Frankie and J.J. didn't get along. By this time, we'd finally gotten J.J. to take the project seriously and address our concerns. Frankie just wanted the contract signed.

Seeing what was happening, Samuel, Jodi, Dan-the-Man and I got very explicit about the deal. We created attachments to the contract that contained metrics Vaporcon would be held to. Additionally, since we had not seen the actual application, we created a design of what it should look like and spelled out its exact functionality. This, too, went into the contract as an attachment.

We had two more concerns. First, we now believed that Vaporcon did not have the resources or know-how to implement a pilot with 500 physicians. Our primary objective for the program was to acquire knowledge. If we went with 500 doctors, Vaporcon would likely spend all its time recruiting and zero time implementing. Instead, I told them to focus on less than 50 physicians in two cities—one wired and the other not. San Francisco and Memphis were selected.

Our second concern was that the Vaporcon application might add another layer between our customers and us. Instead of bringing us closer to doctors and their patients, we could find ourselves shut off from them should Vaporcon at some future time limit our access to their system. If we weren't careful, Vaporcon could easily claim our customers as their own. A smaller pilot meant we could keep a closer eye on things and adjust accordingly to avoid this situation.

The 50-customer pilot was a big turnoff to Vaporcon. They told us that the price—into the seven figures—wasn't going to change just because we were using fewer customers. Actually, the price did come down a little after Samuel finished with them. It would, however, still be a very expensive learning experience on a per-customer basis. A positive return on investment would be virtually impossible.

Frankie Zee wanted to focus on what would happen after the pilot period. Like so many people involved with dot-coms, he was interested in laying down as much track as possible, as soon as possible. Since there was a high likelihood that they hadn't even built the application— something that was becoming more apparent every day—we didn't want to discuss what would happen after the pilot until we could evaluate the results. Frankie was insistent about discussing activities post-pilot. "Look," I said, "we'll cross that bridge when we come to it."

Finally, after well over 100 hours of negotiating, we agreed on a contract. None of us was really happy with the deal, but it was a deal nonetheless. The project was to go live on March 15, which gave Vaporcon about 6 weeks to complete the "finishing touches" on the application and recruit participants. It was an aggressive timeline, but they had assured us they could deliver.

Just prior to the signing, when it was clear we had a deal, I remember Becky saying, "Once the contract's completed, we'll probably never look at it again."

I hoped she didn't actually believe that. From her perspective, she may have seen the contract as some sort of formality. From our perspective, it would serve as the guiding framework for the months ahead.

It was at this time that I decided to oversee the implementation of the project.

There are two schools of thought on who should implement an agreement. One school says that you bring in someone who was not involved with the negotiating process, in case there's bad blood between the two parties. The other school takes the opposite view. They recommend having a person who was intimately involved in the contracting process. The reason being that this person knows the intent behind the contractual language.

Given what I learned from the Hypemeister.com deal, I felt it best if I didn't pass the ball on this one. The bottom line was that I didn't trust Vaporcon.

Soon after the contract was signed, I approved the paperwork for Vaporcon's seven-figure check. They wanted the money in a lump-sum payment up front. The night that our payment was mailed to them, I was at home doing some work online. By chance, I came across a press release issued earlier that evening—after the markets had closed—by Vaporcon's acquiring company.

The release blandly stated that the company had cumulative losses from the year before of over $24 million on revenues of less than $5 million. Further, losses in the most recent quarter were around $10 million on revenue of less than $2 million.

I read and re-read the release, unable to believe it was true. The new company was a money-losing turd. With each reading, my anger rose. I hadn't been this upset since the consultants left my binder in the taxi.

The next morning, I called Vaporcon and demanded to speak immediately with their CEO. Within the hour, Becky had arranged for me to speak not with their CEO, but with their attorney and their head of investor relations. J.J. and Frankie were also on the call.

"Let me be blunt," I told them, "I just read your press release last night and I'm very concerned that you're about to go belly up. I've just sent you a check for seven figures. Are you going bankrupt even before this project gets off the ground?"

Suddenly, there was hysterical laughter. Not from the people at Vaporcon, but from my colleagues sitting in the cubicles around me. They had been listening in on my conversation.

"Did you *really* think they were going to tell you they were going under, even if they were?" one of my peers later chided me.

Sure enough, the Vaporcon folks assured me that they were in solid financial shape. "We've got enough money in the bank to last us at least another 12 months and we have contingency plans in place." I wasn't convinced of the explanation, but it was all I had to go on. My cube mates were right. What was I going to do?

As the implementation phase of the project began, the real fun started. It soon became clear that Vaporcon had an application that was, at best, 10% developed, nowhere close to the 80% they had represented to us in the preceding months. There was no way they could possibly meet the March 15 start-up date as agreed to in the contract.

They also needed to hire additional people. This included two sales representatives in the cities where the pilot was to occur. The sales reps would recruit the 50 physicians needed for the pilot. Additionally, Vaporcon would need a new project manager—the one they had assigned to the job had abruptly resigned. Another person who was to work on the project jumped ship for, ironically, Deluxe-health.com, the company that Outpatient-clinic.com supposedly had the exclusive agreement with. Lastly, another person had to leave due to "medical reasons."

All of this paled in comparison with the next Vaporcon departure. J.J. called me one day to say he had left the company to start his own business. "Don't worry," he told me, "you're in good hands with Frankie Zee."

The only Vaporcon person who was there during the entire negotiation process was now gone.

Although Becky had attended all the meetings, I never really thought she completely grasped the project. My worst fears would soon be confirmed. During one of our frequent calls, Becky confided that she wasn't a "computer girl" and didn't really "get this technical stuff."

A few weeks later, in March, Vaporcon recruited a new project manager, Diane Benoit. Diane was one of those people who diplomatically would be called a very self-assured person. Bluntly, and perhaps unfairly, she might be called ruthless. Regardless of how one viewed her, the key thing to understand was that she lived by the rule, "my way or the highway."

The first meeting Diane participated in was held at our office. A variety of people from my company were in attendance, including Jodi McAdams, the attorney who had helped negotiate the Vaporcon deal.

Diane apparently had two objectives. First, show that she was in charge. Second, demonstrate her facilitation skills. She was the sort of person who gravitated immediately to the markers and white board. This meeting was to be no exception.

Diane, who didn't come from our industry, wanted to show us that she understood it. She didn't disappoint. Upon being introduced, she immediately got up and went to the white board.

"In order for this project to work," she informed us, "we'll need to establish a framework for viewing how your customers make decisions. Then we'll target various points along this decision-process with our application."

And with that she began diagramming our proprietary "Transaction Tool." The exact same tool we had shown to Becky and J.J. at perhaps our third meeting together. Only now, Diane had given it a different name.

"What I'm drawing on the board is something we've developed called the 'Decision Tool.'"

I couldn't believe it. Vaporcon had unabashedly stolen our intellectual property. I was about to say something when Jodi McAdams beat me to the punch. As mentioned previously, Jodi was a fun-loving person, except when she thought someone was taking advantage of Frederick Gold. She thought this was the case now.

"Excuse me, Diane, but what you've written up there is word-for-word our 'Transaction Tool'—not your so-called 'Decision Tool.' What's worse, the term 'Decision Tool' is a trademarked term by our firm. As such, I demand that you immediately cease from using both the Transaction Tool and the name you've associated with it—whether you're talking with us or others."

"I beg your pardon," Diane countered. "This is common knowledge. Anyone could come up with the concept."

"The fact is," I jumped in, "we were the ones who came up with it and we shared it with J.J. and Becky."

I looked over at Becky for confirmation of this fact. She refused to make eye contact, instead choosing to look down at her laptop computer.

"I think we disagree with your account of the events," Diane responded casually.

"Not another word out of your mouth!" It was Jodi, who was quickly escalating the discussion to another level.

"I just told you these are our concepts and that you will stop using them. There is no more discussion. This is very serious. You may not respect the property rights of others, but we do. Now, you will stop using our trademarked name and claiming this idea as your own. Is this clear? If not, I'll be glad to put it in writing for you and discuss it in court. We will vigorously defend our trademarks."

This took the wind out of Diane's sails. She agreed that her firm would comply with Jodi's request, although this didn't stop Jodi from following up with a written notice to their CEO.

The Diane Incident was further confirmation that the people we had gotten into bed with would soon be giving us the business equivalent of syphilis.

The ethics of Vaporcon were indeed lacking. For them to represent our propriety model as their own was disturbing. I never did confront

Becky about it. I didn't need to. The look on her face when we stepped outside for a short cooling off period clearly indicated her guilt.

Although Vaporcon, like Hypemeister.com, was hoping we were going to share our industry expertise with them, we did not. We had never intended to. After the attempted theft of the "Transaction Tool," we agreed to play it very close to the vest. If Vaporcon really had something to offer, let them show us. We weren't about to part with any more of our ideas.

Becky's comment about not paying much attention to the signed contract became prophetic. As we went back and forth on the project specification document, Vaporcon constantly tried to redefine what we had previously agreed to. It was the right decision to keep me involved with the implementation and not hand the project off to someone else. Had another person stepped in, Vaporcon might have gotten away with their proposed changes, which were clearly not mutually beneficial.

After numerous revisions to bring the project spec document in line with our contract, I finally signed off on it. Around this time, Vaporcon invited us to a fancy hotel in New York City for a one-day "Summit." The purpose was for us to meet their executives and to hear about another "blockbuster idea" they had developed. Gerald Hogan and I made the trip.

Their mega-idea was interesting, but like the application they had supposedly developed for us, we weren't sure if it really existed. By this time, Vaporcon had already missed the first set of deadlines on the project and didn't appear to be at all close to meeting the revised deliverable date. Now, they had the nerve to ask if we would cough up even more money for another project.

Gerald inquired if we couldn't just include the proposed idea with our existing project. Frankie Zee, who was leading this particular meeting, said that wasn't possible. The application that they were telling us about today required a different operating platform.

I told Frankie his firm had a little problem. All of the applications that they were developing should be interchangeable with existing applications. They couldn't all be riding on different platforms. It would not only be cost-prohibitive, but a functional nightmare.

In fact, Gerald and I were calling Frankie's bluff. All he was looking for was additional money. The new application could have easily been designed to reside on our application—after all, our application was just now being built.

Frankie said he'd get back to us. He needed to see if he could piggyback the new offering onto the one they were building for us. A few weeks later he sent an e-mail saying that it couldn't be done.

By now, things really started to get bad. Our revised May 1 deadline came and went, as did the June 15 deadline.

The two Vaporcon sales reps were having difficulty signing up customers. This was perfectly understandable. Their only sales tools were some PowerPoint slides, a smile and a shoeshine. I was astounded that they were able to get five physicians to buy in, sight unseen, to the project. Maybe it was because the offering was free to them; they probably viewed it as a no-lose situation. If they didn't like the application, they'd just stop using it.

Given what I viewed as nothing short of incompetence by Vaporcon, not to mention their outright dishonesty, I found it increasingly difficult to deal with them in a civil manner. They couldn't be trusted. Each and every issue we'd brought up during the negotiations was now coming home to roost. During one phone call, Becky told me that they had a situation where there were four physicians in one location, but only three of them were customers of interest to us. The fourth one, however, wanted to participate in the pilot. What should Vaporcon do, she wondered?

I reminded her that I had asked that same question of her and J.J. several months earlier while we were negotiating. The response was that they would deal with it if it became an issue.

"I don't know," I said. "What *are* you going to do?"

They decided to bring on the fourth physician. I told them that was fine, but we weren't going to pay for the inclusion of the additional doctor. Vaporcon agreed.

During another memorable phone conversation, around the June 15 deadline, I was informed of another "risk factor." This term was a euphemism Vaporcon had come up with that meant they had identified another problem, but didn't have an answer for it. They simply wanted to make me "aware" of it. In this instance, the risk factor was that they might not be able to have timely installation of high-speed DSL lines for our customers.

"No problem," I told them. "Run the system on dial-up lines. It may operate a little slower, but it'll work until you get the DSL."

"But you demanded broadband lines for the project. The application can't run on dial-up lines, it wasn't designed for them," Diane said.

"What are you talking about?" I snapped. After months of games, this was the final straw.

"I never said any such thing. J.J. wanted the broadband because he felt it would be an added feature to help make the system more appealing to our customers. I never asked for broadband."

There was silence. Suddenly, emotions that I'd been holding back for months now came exploding out of my mouth.

"You know something, you people are a pain in the ass. This whole project is a pain in the ass. It's been nothing but lies and delays. Let's be honest here. You don't have an application. You didn't have an application when we negotiated the contract and, if you did, there is no way it was 80% built. You people are a bunch of liars. I've got a lot of other work to be focusing on aside from spending nearly all my time babysitting you. I'm tired of this crap. Let's just focus on doing what we've agreed to in the contract."

There was silence on the phone—and in my office. I hadn't merely said all of the above; I had shouted it.

There were probably five Vaporcon people on the line, but only Diane spoke.

"We are honest people and I resent you calling us liars. We've been dealt a bad hand. That doesn't mean that we can't be professional."

Dealt a bad hand? She may have viewed it as such. I saw it differently. Namely as deceit by one party toward another on multiple occasions.

I was too spent to argue with them. At that moment, I decided not to fight any more. They were incompetent. It wasn't going to get better—no matter how angry I got and how much I yelled. If the project ever got off the ground, that would be great. However, I wasn't going to devote any more effort to it. From this point forward, I would shift my focus to other priorities.

"Fine. When do you think we should reset our new start date?"

"We were thinking about August 14. That's about eight weeks from now."

"Done. I'll talk with you next week." I hung up. I then pulled up my calendar and typed in the following entry for August 14: "What will the next deadline be when this one comes and goes?"

A couple weeks later, after one of our weekly chats, Becky called to say that she wanted to have Maxine Lancaster, Gerald Hogan and me set aside 15 minutes for an important call the following day. They wanted to give us a heads-up prior to the issuance of a press release.

I thought the worst. The last time they scheduled a call like this was during the negotiations to let us know that they were being acquired. Now, they were probably going to tell us they were closing up shop. The caffeine had finally worn off. There would be no project. The seven-figure amount we'd sent to them would be gone forever, written off to a costly learning experience.

As it turned out, the news was bad, but not quite fatal. Vaporcon would be laying off about fifty percent of its workforce and terminating an entire line of business. They claimed this would in no way impact our project.

What could I do? Even if it was a lie, my options were limited.

Several weeks later, around August 1, I was enjoying a beautiful summer afternoon at a company-sponsored golf outing when my cell phone rang. I recognized the phone number as Becky's. Why I answered I still don't know. She informed me that the DSL installation "risk factor" had become a reality. This meant that they wouldn't have DSL installed for our customers by the August 14 release date. Once again, we would have to delay our launch.

The new deadline for starting the pilot was September 1—a full six months after it was supposed to begin.

I could only imagine what would have happened had we gone with the entire 500 physicians Vaporcon initially proposed for the pilot. Back then, we were concerned about being cut off from our customers. Now, our primary concern was not disappointing them.

As a dot-com, Vaporcon had little to lose. They had no credibility. However, my company faced the distinct possibility of having its reputation tarnished in the eyes of our customers—even if it was just the 50 who chose to participate in the pilot. For us, each customer is important. At the end of the day, we'd have to rebuild these relationships. Vaporcon would most likely be filing for Chapter 11.

There is a pathetic epilogue to the story.

J.J., the person who sold us the "80% built application" recently called. He wanted to tell me how his new start-up company was doing. I should have hung up, but I listened politely.

He was apparently selling banner advertisements for a group of Web sites and wanted to know if I was interested in buying some spots for my company. I explained that I viewed banner ads as virtually worthless expenditures, since the click-through rates were less than one percent—and falling.

Undaunted, J.J. then invited me to a golf tournament with "important people" in my industry. The tournament was to be held in New

York State. He would cover my greens fees, but "because I'm a small start-up," he told me, "you'll have to pay your own way out here."

J.J. and I have not spoken since that call. I've instructed my administrative assistant to never put him through to me again.

CHAPTER 11
JUST THE FACTS, MA'AM

The Hypemeister.com and Vaporcon deals were big disappointments. But they were also good learning experiences. In the past, I may have given a vendor the benefit of the doubt when something didn't sound quite right. After all, I didn't want to look stupid by asking what appeared to be dumb questions. Those days were long gone. It was bad enough when people couldn't deliver on a promise. I now had little tolerance for people who were less than forthright from the start.

A case-in-point is a company called "ClinicKiosk.com." Their sales guy made it through to Gerald Hogan's voicemail. Gerald immediately forwarded the call on to me. By doing so, Gerald was following our commitment to route all vendor inquiries to one person. In this instance it paid off.

As previously mentioned, I keep copious notes for all my contacts with vendors. I do this mostly because my memory isn't very good and because I speak with so many people, it's easy to confuse one with another.

Here is a portion of the notes that I transcribed from the ClinicKiosk.com person's phone call to Gerald:

"We have 1,000 Internet-linked computer kiosks up and running in clinics today [April 2000]. We'll have 2,000 kiosks by the end of the year."

When I called the ClinicKiosk.com rep three days later, he told me that they had "500 kiosks running today" and that they'd have "1,000 by September," which he immediately modified to June. Obviously, there was a big discrepancy between what he told me and what he told Gerald. In my notes, I wrote the following: "He's loose with his numbers. Be careful."

"500 or 1,000 kiosks—what does it matter?" the ClinicKiosk.com guy must have thought. Well, to me, it matters quite a bit. I asked him to send me some written information, figuring he'd leave me alone. He would hear none of it. Finally, I had him book a visit for a month later. If his company were still around, I'd give him an hour of my time.

Sure enough, he showed up as scheduled. He went through the benefits of the application, which, unlike Vaporcon's, did exist. I again pressed him for the number of kiosks actually in use. He continued to be vague.

I told him that we'd been burned in the past. Although I personally didn't think patients would use his offering, I was willing to keep an open mind. The only way that I could think of to see if people would use it, was to visit—unannounced—some of the clinics where he claimed it was operating so I could get a first-hand account. I asked if he would please send me a list of the locations.

"No problem," he said. He'd take care of this as soon as he returned to the office. As we finished our meeting, he reiterated something he said to Gerald and to me previously: This was a limited, exclusive sponsorship opportunity. If we didn't accept, he was in deep negotiations with a competitor that were close to being completed. He didn't think the opportunity would be available in another two weeks. I told him that I appreciated his informing me of this fact, but that I wanted to see patients using his computer kiosk with my own eyes before I made a decision. This discussion occurred on May 15.

On June 6, the Kiosk rep called to say he'd signed up a competitor in another category. "Congratulations," I told him. "By the way, I asked, "how's my list of locations coming along? I still haven't received it yet."

"Don't worry," he said, "it's on the way."

One month later, on July 6, the list still hadn't arrived. However, I learned from some people in our U.S. division that the ClinicKiosk.com rep had chosen to bypass me and start talking directly with our brand teams. This was exactly the type of situation we had hoped to avoid. Here was a person who was getting nowhere fast with me because I was looking to verify the facts. Instead, he decided to search for the weak links in our organization. He was successful with at least two of our brand teams, who expressed an interest.

I suppose the ClinicKiosk.com guy never thought I'd find this out, or find it out too late. He probably thought that even if I did find out, that he could talk his way out of it. It never occurred to him that I would contact the CEO of his company to discuss the matter directly. Which is what I did.

When I explained the situation to the CEO, he listened and said he'd look into it. "Fine," I told him. "Until you get back in touch with me, I don't want your guy contacting anyone at my company." He agreed.

A day later the CEO called back. His explanation was that his account rep had supposedly tried on three separate occasions to e-mail the location list to me, but that it didn't go through. At that point, I interrupted him.

"Let's look at what you're telling me. Your representative says he's sent me the list three times via e-mail. This directly contradicts what he's told me. But let's assume that he really did send the list and that he had a bad e-mail address. I gave him one of my business cards during our meeting. My card has my correct e-mail address on it. Fine, let's assume your guy's eyesight is poor and he can't read my business card. Wouldn't he call me after he got a 'mail undeliverable' notice so he could confirm the e-mail address? As an absolute last resort, couldn't he have sent a hardcopy of the list via FedEx, which would have required my signature, to confirm I received it? Is your employee's behavior acceptable to you?"

I never got an answer to the question. Later that day, however, the CEO e-mailed the list to me. He also followed up by phone to confirm I'd received it. I now knew why they were hesitant to send a list. It was a mess. Not only were there incomplete addresses, but also duplicate addresses and addresses that didn't exist. I took 30 minutes to clean the list and could only find 278 locations. Far fewer than the 500 or 1,000 that had been represented to us previously.

Now that I know the facts about ClinicKiosk.com, I'm in no hurry to conduct my in-person visit, despite the weekly calls from the company offering their assistance to "set me up" at one of their locations.

Ironically, in their most recent phone call, they offered us a free trial program. Funny, I guess that competitor of ours who was "this close" to signing with them four months ago never materialized.

It's a shame, really. ClinicKiosk.com tried to take the easy way out, instead of giving me the facts up front. I have no doubt they'll find another taker, but it won't be my firm. They've unfortunately raised the bar for every other company that tries to come through our door.

CHAPTER 12
CLOSE, BUT NO CIGAR

By this point, I wondered if we would ever encounter an honest New Economy company. Our criteria seemed simple enough. We sought a firm that would keep its word *and* have a functioning product or service. In June, it appeared that our prayers had been answered.

Everything seemed right about DocDevice.com. The people we met had integrity. This alone differentiated them from just about everyone else we'd come across in the last several months. Even better, DocDevice's objectives and ours were aligned.

Unlike Hypemeister.com, this was not a shotgun marriage. Both parties were walking hand-in-hand to the altar.

Our discussions with DocDevice.com were refreshing. Instead of deluging us with New Economy jargon, they spoke in plain English. Perhaps this was because the company was headquartered in a small town far away from Silicon Valley.

The company's CEO and founder, Bobby Quinn, was a hands-on technologist. He and his team had developed a novel way to transmit information wirelessly. Bobby believed his technology would be useful for physicians, who spend much of their day going from one exam room to the next. Bobby's technology would enable doctors to complete several routine tasks more efficiently. In turn, he thought, doctors could then spend more time with their patients.

We liked the concept and wanted to explore it further. Allen Ackerman, the Global e-Commerce group's resident "techie," assessed the system. His conclusion was that it showed merit. He cautioned us, however, that we were dealing with something on the cutting edge—or even, he said, on the bleeding edge. This meant the technology was not perfect. We would, Allen assured us, discover problems with it.

After carefully weighing the possible benefits and risks, we decided to move forward.

For several days, Bobby's attorney and business development person met with Dan-the-Man, Luke Stone and me to craft a deal. In contrast to our negotiations with Outpatient-clinic.com, Hypemeister.com and Vaporcon, our sessions with DocDevice.com were acrimony-free. As a result, we quickly came to general terms on an eight-month pilot project. Our goal was to see how the technology performed in the real world. If it worked as advertised, we would consider expanding to a larger scale.

Just when I thought we had a deal, DocDevice.com dropped an eleventh-hour bomb.

As we went over the specific terms of the agreement, Bobby and his people said repeatedly that they wanted the majority of the seven-figure amount to be delivered up front. We were uncomfortable with this and told them so. Nevertheless, they were insistent.

Red flags started to go up immediately. We'd been burned with our up-front payment to Vaporcon. I was determined not to let that happen again.

Luke Stone, our Harvard MBA, opened up the DocDevice.com prospectus to have a closer look. Given his workload, Luke hadn't been able to research the deal in depth. To his horror, he discovered that the company had only $1.5 million in cash on hand. A paltry amount, given the so-called "burn rate" at which most dot-com enterprises spend their money.

"How much do you have in the bank today?" Luke asked.

"Under two million dollars," replied Bobby's attorney.

"What's your burn rate?"

"Five hundred thousand a month."

My stomach clenched. It was suddenly clear to us why they were so insistent to have the money up front. The company had just four months to live unless it got immediate funding. We were once again going to be the zero-interest lender. Our concern was that DocDevice.com wouldn't have enough money to see them through the eight months of our pilot. Bobby's attorney knew we had just uncovered a potential deal-killer.

"Look, this is not a problem," he said. "We can get money from venture capital firms any time we want. It's just that the terms aren't favorable right now. We want to borrow as little as possible and only when we need it. We'll wait for the market to pick up again."

It sounded plausible. But what if the market didn't pick up? It was summer 2000 and the technology-laden Nasdaq had been in the doldrums for months. There were no signs this situation was going to change anytime soon.

Given our recent experiences, we refused to make a large up front payment. There was too much risk involved. Instead, Luke Stone suggested disbursing money when DocDevice.com obtained additional financing from another source, such as a bank or venture capital firm.

The idea was to pay DocDevice.com only if they received funding in an amount equal to or greater than what they sought from us. Such a strategy would give them an incentive to find additional financing, which would reduce their risk of bankruptcy during our pilot. Unfortunately, this idea did not appeal to them. They felt it would force them to accept onerous terms from other possible financing sources.

Because we believed in Bobby and his technology, we continued to search for a mutually agreeable solution. If DocDevice.com continued to play hardball, however, we were prepared to walk away. We were not going to relive the Vaporcon situation.

Our next suggestion was for tiered payments. These would start low and then increase to ever-larger amounts as Bobby and his team met explicit milestones at various stages of the project. In this way, we'd be able to structure our outlay so that more money would be paid at the end of the contract—provided we made it to the end of the project. If DocDevice.com was unable to meet any of the pre-determined objectives, the agreement would be terminated.

The tiered payments solution was brought up during a phone call in which Maxine Lancaster participated. To everyone's relief, DocDevice.com agreed to the terms. After the call, Maxine again uttered her famous line, "I think we're there, guys." This time, she was right.

I continued working with DocDevice.com as we transitioned from the negotiation phase to the implementation phase. About three weeks into the project, I got a first-hand look at what it was like to work with bleeding edge technology.

We had selected a local clinic as the first site to install and test Bobby's equipment. Almost from the beginning, the wireless transmission system acted erratically in its real world setting. Every so often the system would simply stop transmitting, which didn't exactly please the doctors.

At first, no one knew why. After spending a day at the clinic, however, a technician from DocDevice.com realized there was a pattern to the system failures. If the doctor was in the front of the office, the system worked fine. If she was in the back, the signal tended to be intermittent.

The conundrum was solved when the technician discovered an x-ray machine in a room separating the front of the office from the back. At first, he thought the x-ray machine might be causing the problem. Then he realized it wasn't the machine, but the room itself.

To protect medical workers and others from prolonged exposure to radiation, x-ray machines are housed in lead-enclosed rooms. Lead-lined walls inhibit the transmission of x-rays beyond the room. Of course, a lead-lined wall also prevents the transmission of other signals—such as the radio frequency used by Bobby's equipment.

Bobby's team had placed a small transmission antenna in the front part of the office. This antenna sent a wireless radio signal to the device Bobby had provided to each doctor. If the doctor was in the front of the office, everything worked fine. However, if the lead walls of the x-ray machine room came between the doctor and the antenna, the transmission failed.

The problem was easily solved when additional antennas were installed around the x-ray room. Now, the system worked regardless of where the physicians were in their office. Everyone was happy.

For a few weeks, I didn't hear much from DocDevice.com. Then one day Bobby called. He was quite excited. After months of research, his team had developed a primitive voice recognition feature for the system. We had known he was working on this and were quite anxious to see his progress. He invited us for a demonstration. I flew out the next morning with a colleague from our U.S. Division.

Upon our arrival at DocDevice.com's office, we were lead to the main conference room. Inside were Bobby's attorney and the business development person. They both looked a little ill. I spoke with them for a few minutes until Bobby made his appearance. He was carrying a small device in one hand, which he nearly dropped in his haste to greet my colleague and me.

"Brian, I'm so glad you were able to come on such short notice. Please, please have a seat."

He indicated that I should sit across from his attorney and business development person. As Bobby walked to the head of the table, I noticed that something was different about him. Normally, he was a very mellow person. Today, he appeared almost manic.

"As you know," Bobby said, speaking very fast, "we've been working for a while now to get a voice recognition feature built into the system. I'm pleased to announce that we've succeeded."

"That's great," I told him, "we're interested to see a demonstration."

"Well, you won't be disappointed."

And with that he flipped open the cover to the small handheld computer he had carried into the room.

"This is the same device we're testing with the doctors over at the clinic. The only difference is that now it responds to voice commands. From now on, the doctors don't need to type in the patient's name. They just speak it."

Bobby looked at my colleague and I for confirmation.

"Sounds cool," I said. "Let's see it in action."

Bobby picked up the device and held it about a foot away from his mouth.

"I need to have it fairly close to me so other sounds in the room aren't picked up by the microphone. Let's assume the patient's name is John Doe. I simply press this button and speak the name. The system will automatically pull up Mr. Doe's information."

We all leaned forward as Bobby pressed the button and in a normal voice said, "John Doe." He released the button and looked at the screen. Apparently, whatever was supposed to happen didn't.

"Hmmm," he said, looking a little puzzled, "let me try it again."

This time he moved the computer to within six inches of his face and said "John Doe" very slowly.

Nothing.

I glanced over at the DocDevice attorney and business development person. They looked like they'd rather be anywhere else on earth right now.

"I don't understand," said Bobby. "This was working fine a moment ago. There must be some interference in this room."

I suppressed the urge to ask if there were any lead walls in DocDevice's newly-built office.

"Maybe it's because we're quite a distance from the base station and antenna," Bobby theorized. "Let's walk a little closer to the base station."

And with that, he rose and motioned for us to follow him. My colleague and I got up, but the attorney and business development person remained seated.

We walked out of the conference room and into the reception area.

"Let's try it again," said Bobby. He pressed the button and in a deliberate voice said, "John Doe." He released the button. Again, nothing happened. He examined the device from all sides and then shook it a little.

"This is really odd. Let's go a little closer."

And so it went as we walked around his offices. Bobby would speak the words "John Doe" into the microphone and then wait for the screen to bring up Mr. Doe's information. Nothing would happen. He'd take another few steps and repeat the process. Apparently, the sight of the CEO speaking the words "John Doe" into a small computer was a common occurrence at DocDevice.com. None of the employees we walked passed bothered to look up from their work.

After perhaps six attempts, the system finally cooperated.

"Ah, there we go," said a relieved Bobby. "The screen has John Doe's information on it."

He turned the device around so I could see. It did indeed have Mr. Doe's information.

"I suppose we've got a little work to do before we show this feature at the medical technology conference next week" Bobby admitted. By now, his initial mania had all but disappeared.

Such is life with technology on the cutting edge. I didn't mind. Allen Ackerman told us the technology wasn't perfect. We had in fact entered the deal with our eyes wide open.

Ironically, we began to have problems with DocDevice.com for reasons other than technology glitches.

Given the bear market in technology stocks, Bobby was finding it increasingly difficult to secure additional financing on terms he liked. Instead of devoting time to the pilot program, Bobby and his management team were consumed with keeping his privately held company solvent. Our worst-case scenario was now playing out. Thankfully, the contract was structured such that our risk was limited only to the small amount of money we had paid up-front.

When DocDevice.com missed the first milestone spelled out in our agreement, we told them the relationship was finished. They pleaded with us to give them another chance. Technically, we weren't required to do so. However, because we believed in their technology, we gave them a five-day extension to satisfy the requirement. At the end of the five days, they asked for more time. We declined and the pilot program was terminated.

Make no mistake. This was a tough decision. We really did believe in DocDevice.com. On several occasions, investment-banking firms would call us during their due diligence efforts. We expressed our support of the company and its technology. Sadly, the capital market's tolerance for risk had dropped dramatically in the past six months. As a result, DocDevice.com was forced to live day by day.

I still keep in touch with a few folks at Bobby's company. Each time we talk, they tell me they're on the verge of getting financing. Yet, it never seems to materialize. I'm optimistic that one day they will find other interested parties. And when that day comes, I'll look forward to discussing the re-launch of our pilot project with them.

CHAPTER 13
CONFERENCES

Conferences that focus on dot-coms, the Internet and the New Economy are a hoot. I've been to them in all parts of the country and it's always the same story—a bunch of people running around claiming that they have the next Big Thing.

Essentially, these conferences boil down to little more than expensive vendor lovefests held in beautiful locations.

Day One of these events starts with everyone trying to out-hype each other. During Day Two, the event turns into a group therapy session with everyone commiserating about why nobody "out there" in the Old Economy understands how great their ideas are. Day Three generally ends with everyone telling each other how wonderful they are and that the Promised Land of fame and fortune is just around the corner.

I attended several conferences when I began my e-commerce job. Once I started seeing the same people time and time again, I caught onto the game. I think other Old Economy firms have as well. Very few Old Economy companies attend these events. Every conference I've gone to has consisted almost entirely of unknown dot-coms.

The situation can really get bad when the scheduled speakers don't show up. In years past when I attended conferences on other subjects, it was a rare occurrence that a speaker was a no-show. At Internet-related events, it's an expectation.

Speakers at these conferences usually pay their own way. So why would they go? They view the conference as an opportunity to hype their company to a captive audience.

The organizers of most conferences line up their speakers several weeks ahead of time. Unfortunately, "several weeks" is the equivalent of "years" for an Internet company. In many instances, the caffeine has started to wear off between the date that the speaker commits and the date of the conference. What's a speaker to do? Since he doesn't receive any compensation, he simply doesn't show up. After all, what has he got to lose?

Conference organizers have gotten quite creative when it comes to explaining why a scheduled presenter is not available. The excuses tend to romanticize the situation. An example might be, "Bob X of Mega-Hypster.com was to join us today, but he chose instead to stay at the office. Bob is leading the charge to land a big account."

In reality, Bob is probably one step ahead of his creditors and doing all he can to avoid having the electricity shut off.

If a presenter isn't using the conference to hype his own company, chances are he's taking the opportunity to publicly disparage his competitors. Many Old Economy firms don't engage in this behavior at public forums. Dot-coms, however, have no qualms about doing so.

One specific example of competitor-bashing occurred at a conference I attended in November 1999. The speaker had worked at a well-known dot-com firm, but recently left to start his own company. This was his first opportunity to talk with a large audience about his new venture. He started his presentation by citing all the weaknesses of his former employer. This continued for perhaps fifteen of the slides in his thirty-slide presentation.

He then went on to speak about his company and why it was better. He was a very slick presenter. Although he *said* his company was better, in reality it was an identical copy of the company he had worked for previously. The business model was pretty much the same, as was the intended customer.

When he finished, the audience roared with approval. He then asked if there were questions from the audience. I went to one of the microphones and said, "You've spent a lot of time talking about why your former company won't succeed. However, your company's business model is essentially identical to that of your prior employer. Given the similarities, aren't you in fact telling us that your new company is doomed to failure?"

Well, Mr. Slick didn't miss a trick. Without losing his composure, he replied, "That's like asking me how often I beat my wife." The audience loved the quick-witted response. He then followed up with a nonsensical answer about why his company was different. Essentially, his premise was that if he said it was different, then dammit, it was different.

If he wanted to, he could have sold shares at a hundred dollars each to the thousand or so people in attendance. They probably would have paid double. The last time I checked, his new venture had gone nowhere.

One other conference story is worth noting. It involves an executive from a well-known Old Economy company who spoke at an Internet gathering. His employer has been in business for over a century and is the subject of numerous Business School case studies—about the right way to run a firm.

He spoke to a standing-room-only crowd in the cavernous ballroom of a Manhattan hotel. The gentleman was clearly a seasoned professional with many years of experience and lessons learned. The audience listened attentively.

When he finished, he took a handful of questions from the crowd. The one I remember most came from a woman who was in her thirties. How, she wondered, does a dot-com company like hers establish credibility?

The way she asked it implied there was a simple, overnight solution to building a reputation and creating customer trust.

To his credit, the executive didn't smirk, laugh or appear to be taken aback. He said simply, "My company's been in business over 100 years..." and let his voice trail off. Credibility, he implied, was earned over time. You just didn't have it bestowed upon you.

The woman's question is a sign of our times. Many people, especially those involved in the New Economy, assume most everything can be achieved in an accelerated fashion. Credibility, however, can not. There's no such thing as "instant credibility."

It takes a long time to establish trust. We're talking lasting relationships here—not one-night stands. Sadly, although credibility takes a long time to achieve, it can be lost literally overnight.

Which brings us to one reason why Internet companies want to "partner" with the Old Economy companies they are so quick to dismiss as dinosaurs. These successful Old Economy firms have something the dot-coms desperately need: Credibility.

SECTION THREE:
ALL ABOUT NEW ECONOMY FIRMS

CHAPTER 14
BROTHER, CAN YOU SPARE A DIME?

Why is it that dot-coms and other so-called New Economy firms even bother to call my company and others in the Old Economy if they think we just "don't get it"?

Two reasons: Money and Credibility—in that order.

In the Old Days, people might tinker around in their garage or den with an idea in their off-hours. They usually funded the endeavor themselves or sought out family and friends for additional financing if needed. Sometimes these entrepreneurs went to banks, but banks charged interest. They could also go to people they didn't know who might give them money. These people, however, usually wanted something in return—like significant ownership. As such, most entrepreneurs chose to go the family and friends route because the cost of borrowing was less—or, as was often the case, free.

Of course, if the idea actually developed into something big, the entrepreneur might not have a choice but to seek larger funding amounts from sources he didn't necessarily like, but saw as a necessary evil.

Today, we have venture capital firms. These folks lend money to individuals and companies they think have an idea that might actually be accepted by the marketplace. To compensate them for the risk they take, VCs either charge an appropriate amount of interest and/or take an equity position in the start-up. They may also provide other services, such as installing a management team.

I'm making this all very simple to drive home a point: Nothing mystical is going on when it comes to borrowing money. The basic laws of finance that have been around for centuries are still in effect.

Today, many entrepreneurs believe that they must work at Internet Speed. When it comes to financing, they interpret this to mean getting large amounts of capital quickly to promote their ideas—no matter how half-baked they are. Well, VC partners are no dummies. They generally don't make uninformed decisions about where to invest their money; they're going to ask for something in return for taking the risk.

Of course, many dot-coms have their requests rejected by VCs, the banks and, sometimes, even family and friends. Where are they to go for financing?

If you said profitable Old Economy companies, you'd be right.

Dot-coms and entrepreneurs don't view me so much as a business development person as they do a zero-interest lender. Almost every one of the ten to fifteen calls that I take from dot-coms and dreamers each day comes down to the same bottom line: A request for money—interest-free, thank you.

Because my firm is profitable, those who contact me are under the apparent misconception that I have "extra" money just burning a hole in my pocket. I don't. And even if this were the case, I don't give away money without asking for something in return. With the possible exceptions of one's parents and the United Way, no one just gives out "free" money.

To be fair, when our e-commerce group first started, we were a little more naive about how we looked at possible deals. The marketplace was in its infancy and we took more risk than was prudent. Today, the marketplace has matured. Unless a dot-com or entrepreneur is coming to me with a concept that actually exists and has customers that I can visit, I'm not interested. Sorry, bank closed.

Even if the product or service exists and is being used, I'm still going to ask hard questions and conduct my due diligence. If my findings indicate that there's something of value, we may negotiate a deal. However, the transaction is structured so that it's performance-based. After all, there's no such thing as a free lunch—even in the New Economy.

Aside from money, the other reason dot-coms come to my firm is for credibility. Most every Internet enterprise I talk to tells me that they want to "partner" with my company. Let's assume for a moment that they really don't want my money. If this is indeed the case, then what they want is the credibility that my firm brings to the party.

Dot-coms want to partner with established companies that have strong brand names. Today, these companies, which consumers trust and find credible, tend to be Old Economy firms. I often ask Internet companies how much *they* should pay me for the privilege of utilizing my firm's good will. After all, I'm helping them grow *their* business.

The whole concept of partnering is synonymous with "guilt by association." It's kind of like being in high school. If you hang out with the "in crowd," then, by association, you're "in." Of course the in crowd must accept you. Sometimes, the in crowd is unsure about you, but decides to extend the benefit of the doubt. If, after a certain period of time, you don't prove yourself worthy, you'll find yourself out with everyone else.

The same thing happens in the real world when it comes to credibility. If you proclaim your company as standing for something, a certain percentage of the population will give you the benefit of the doubt, for a little while. But if your company doesn't prove its worth, it will find itself in deep trouble. Just ask the many dot-coms who couldn't deliver on their promises and felt the Market's wrath in April 2000.

Wait until the caffeine truly wears off. You'll see exactly what happens to companies that thought they could buy instant credibility.

For businesses fortunate enough to have a good reputation, there's one particularly insidious danger of partnering with an unknown dot-com: The dot-com's actions can easily tarnish the established firm's credibility.

Remember the Vaporcon story? They had no reputation. We did and we paid dearly for their incompetence when it came time to repair the relationships with our customers.

All too often, clueless Old Economy firms pay large amounts of money to New Economy firms for supposed partnership "opportunities." These partnerships do little except build the dot-com's reputation—oftentimes at the expense of the Old Economy firm's reputation.

In essence, the Old Economy firm unknowingly transfers its credibility to the dot-com. Unfortunately, by the time this discovery is made, the Old Economy firm has lost *its* customers to the New Economy firm—*and* paid to do so. Who would do such a thing? Open the *Wall Street Journal* on any given day and you'll find plenty of examples. It takes a long time to build a brand. Do all you can to protect it.

CHAPTER 15
SELLING THE SIZZLE

There's a famous Harvard Business Review article entitled "The Core Competence of the Corporation." A core competence is defined as a "bundle of skills and technologies that enables a company to provide a particular benefit to customers." A classic example of core competence is Sony's ability to design and bring to market innovative electronics products before their competitors do.

What if you're an Internet start-up with a questionable business plan, little funding and a large burn rate? What's your core competency? Selling the sizzle, that's what.

Indeed, at most dot-coms it seems that the first person hired isn't the technology guy or someone with business acumen; rather, it's the public relations hack.

For Internet companies, image is everything. The product or service being promoted is a distant second. In fact, many dot-coms only have a vague idea of the product or service they'd like to sell. Their slick salespeople are looking to you not only for funding, but for input on how to flesh out their ideas—ideas that they will take to your competitors because they know it works.

All of this brings up the question of which comes first in the New Economy: The development of a tangible offering (i.e. a product or service) or the promotion of the offering? This is more than just a theoretical question. It gets to the essence of when and how the caffeine will wear off.

In the Old Economy, building the product or service came first. The formation of a brand came next, based upon the satisfaction and feelings that customers associated with the offering and what it did for them. Branding was secondary. Of primary importance was an offering that delivered on its promise to perform.

Examples of companies that became successful from doing business in this manner include General Electric, Ford and McDonald's. They've existed for many years because they created products and services that people valued. It took several years for these brands to develop.

Today, many people associated with the New Economy cite Starbucks Coffee as a strong brand. Apparently, the implication is that Starbucks came out of nowhere overnight through creative public relations. Go back and look at the history. Starbucks' brand and image developed over a 20-year period by delivering a solid product and experience to its customers. The brand clearly followed the product.

Contrast the companies above with those of the New Economy. Internet firms spend an enormous amount of time and money on branding as opposed to developing a viable product or service. Due to so-called "Internet time compression," dot-com companies apparently feel compelled to establish their name before actually delivering a service.

Many New Economy companies are betting that one day they can actually live up to the promises they're making. It's not dissimilar to the way politicians operate while campaigning—and look at how dissatisfied we are with politics today.

Conversely, in the Old Economy, it was the product or service itself that established the promise with the consumer—not a hastily written press release filled with hyperbole. Today, it really does seem to be a case of the tail wagging the dog.

Indeed, dot-coms are expert at making lofty promises of mutually beneficial "relationships" between themselves and their profitable Old Economy brethren. The constant reference to relationships bothered me during my first few weeks on the job because my definition of a relationship was more Old Economy in nature. Namely, that it implies a long-term commitment between two parties. It was clear to me that the actions of Internet companies indicated that they had no intention of pursuing a long-term partnership.

So why do dot-coms continue to use the term "relationship?" One day it dawned on me while listening to a 27-year old at a branding conference in San Francisco. "Relationship" to a Generation X dot-comer means something entirely different than it does to a baby boomer like me. With the divorce rate for first marriages soaring in the United States, many Gen Xers grew up in families where a long-term relationship between their birth parents did not exist. As a result, the definition of "relationship" is undergoing a change.

Today, relationships apparently mean a lot of intense "wooing," where one's promises may or may not be followed up with action. I wonder if dot-com companies and others who believe the New Economy mantra of "branding first" will merely engage in short-term "flings" rather than serious long-term interactions with consumers.

Will consumers' "divorce rate" with companies that can't deliver on their promises approach that of first marriages? Perhaps no one in Generation X cares. After all, they're just mimicking in business what they've seen in their personal lives. The implications for business, however, will be profound when numerous New Economy companies vanish into the ether.

CHAPTER 16
TURN, TURN, TURN

There is one very tangible manifestation of how the definition of relationship is different today than it was with past generations: Employee turnover.

At large Old Economy firms, it was fairly common for people to spend their entire career with the same company. Today, this is becoming more of a quaint rarity. At New Economy enterprises, it's a laughable absurdity. If the employee isn't getting instant gratification and making "lots of money," he's gone.

At Internet companies, a long-time employee is one who's been there more than six months. I'm not kidding. A few weeks ago, I met with two people who had impressive-sounding titles. The words "we," "us" and "our company" were littered throughout their conversation. Something seemed a little too forced. At one point, I asked how long the guy on my left had been with the company. He said three months. I then turned to the guy on my right and asked how long he'd been with the firm. Two *weeks*, he said—and he was the one doing all the talking.

People leave dot-coms for lots of reasons. They're laid off. They want to pursue different opportunities. Their stock options are worthless. You name it. The bottom line is that there's not much loyalty between employee and employer in the New Economy. Here are two examples. The first is a woman who worked with "Alfuh.com," which competed directly with "Zatuh.com." She called monthly to solicit my business.

Every time, she brutally bashed her competitor. So much so that it turned me off from wanting to talk with her.

One month she phoned, and I asked how it was going at Alfuh. There was a pause. She told me she was no longer at Alfuh. Where did she go? You guessed it. She was now at Zatuh. I burst out laughing. "It's not really such a bad company," she informed me and then started to blast away at her former employer. Talk about a credibility issue. I listened for a few minutes then told her I had to go. We haven't spoken since.

The second example of employment prostitution concerns someone I negotiated with who we'll call "Mr. Big." He was a very articulate—and arrogant—person. Unfortunately, Mr. Big didn't win very many friends with his style. This guy truly worked at Internet speed and couldn't cut deals fast enough. Apparently, a large portion of Mr. Big's compensation was in stock options. If he didn't close his deals, he would be terminated and his stock options could not be exercised.

Fortunately, Mr. Big was successful in securing deals worth hundreds of millions of dollars for his company. As suddenly as it all began, however, the deals stopped coming. I didn't think much about it until a subsequent conversation with someone at another firm. Ironically, the person I was speaking with had also negotiated with Mr. Big. He told me that Mr. Big had cashed in his stock options at the earliest opportunity and abruptly left his place of employment. Where did he go? To a start-up firm he had tried to acquire a few months earlier.

You can say what you want about Mr. Big's loyalty to his previous employer, but he knew when to jump ship. Shortly after he departed, the stock dropped around 80%.

Not surprisingly, immediately after Mr. Big arrived at his new company, a flurry of press releases started flowing about the firm and its product. Prior to knowing Mr. Big had joined their company, I had wondered why the firm was generating so much attention. Now I knew. Mr. Big was again starting to work his magic.

In the New Economy, if you don't see someone from a dot-com for a couple of meetings or don't hear from them for a month or so, don't be too concerned. They'll surface again—often with one of their competitors. Loyalty is a passe concept in the New Economy.

CHAPTER 17
FIDDLING WHILE ROME
BURNS

You might think that a company with a large burn rate and no immediate signs of profitability would be careful about how it spends its money. You would think. But for Internet firms, the bleaker the situation, the more they spend. Apparently, it's a strange manifestation of denial.

Much as Nero is said to have played his fiddle while Rome burned around him, dot-coms tend to distract themselves with a lavish lifestyle. The reasoning must be either 1) "If it were really that bad, we couldn't afford to do this, could we?" or 2) "If we're going down, we might as well have fun." The first statement is told to those outside the company, the second to those inside the company.

There was one firm that loved to take us out for expensive dinners and talk about how they would change the world. They'd secure a lovely wood-paneled private dining room at a local hotel and then order several bottles of expensive wine and more appetizers than 15 people could possibly consume. It was an obscene display of waste, as there were generally only about six of us at any of these intimate gatherings.

My most endearing memory of the three or four meetings that we had with them was that their president loved the pomp and circumstance that went along with fine dining. At our dinner meetings, there was a waiter dedicated to each of us. When the main course arrived, the tuxedoed servers would set the plates down before us, and then with great flourish, simultaneously remove the silver lids covering our entrees. Without fail, the dot-com's president would clap his hands together excitedly like a small child receiving gifts at a birthday party. "Bon appetit!" he would chirp as we began eating.

The dinners continued about every two months, even though the company was clearly facing difficult times. Were they trying to buy our business? Probably. But that's the way Internet firms perceive how the game is played. We didn't sign a deal with them and their president left the company to "pursue other opportunities." We haven't been treated to a dinner at that restaurant since his departure.

Another dot-com I've dealt with appears to have been born with a silver spoon in its mouth. Bottles of wine, hard-to-come-by tickets to sporting events and other gifts have all been proffered. They were all returned or given away.

One time, when they took me out to dinner—at a steak house, of course—I happened to mention that my boss really loved fine coffee, but he couldn't find it here in the States like he could in Europe. Two days later, a European coffee machine and coffee arrived for him at the office. Ask and you shall receive, I suppose. The machine, by the way, sits unused in a corner. It serves as a monument to dot-com excess.

Yet another Internet company whose offices I visited also spent lavishly. They had recently renovated the entire floor of a prestigious building to satisfy their vision of what a successful firm should look like. All of the cubicles were outfitted in a black enamel retro style complete with fashionable gooseneck halogen lamps. The piece de resistance, however, was their kitchen. It resembled a cafe on Park Avenue. There was a commercial grade refrigerator, espresso machine, bar stools and the latest in pseudo wood lounge chairs. The fiftieth floor view was breathtaking.

They lived the high life, right up until the moment one July day when management called everyone into a room and announced that two-thirds of the staff was fired.

In a few weeks, they moved to smaller office space and gave up everything they'd built just three months earlier. No more kitchen and no more caffe lattes. For them, sadly, the caffeine literally wore off.

CHAPTER 18
TRUTH OR DARE

If George Washington did in fact say, "I cannot tell a lie," he would find working at a dot-com difficult. Truth is a rare commodity in the New Economy.

In many of my conversations with Internet-related companies, I feel like an attorney deposing a witness. It's a game of twenty questions to get at the truth. One classic conversation I had concerned a product that was a billed as "hardware and software all in one." Here's how the conversation went:

Caller: "Yes, my device is hardware *and* software."

Me: "I'm not sure I understand. Is it hardware or is it software?"

Caller: "It's both! That's what's so great about it."

Me: "OK. Tell me again how it works."

Caller: "The device plugs into the back of your computer with a standard cable. Whenever your computer is turned on, you can press a button on this device and get connected to the Internet."

Me: "But can't you do that through the computer itself via a browser?"

Caller: "Let me finish. Once you're connected to the Internet, you can press any of ten buttons on the device and be transported directly to one of ten Web pages that you set. Of course, as a sponsor, your company's Web page would be pre-set for one of the buttons. Pressing the button takes the user directly to your site."

Me: "This sounds like the 'favorites' part of a browser. Why wouldn't someone just save their favorite Web sites into their 'favorites?'"

Caller: "You know, a lot of people have difficulty with computers. This saves them time."

Me: "I see."

Caller: "Did I tell you that your mouse can actually sit on top of this device?"

Me: "No."

Caller: "It can! The buttons are flush, so the mouse slides right over them."

Me: "It sounds like what you're describing is a cross between an Internet browser with its favorites and a mouse pad. In fact, it sounds more like a mouse pad with ten buttons on it."

Caller: "It's a hardware-software device."

Me: "I see. How many people are currently using your device?"

Caller: "Not many."

Me: "Can you be more specific?"

Caller: "Actually, I'm building the prototype right now."

Me: "So, no one's actually using your device today?"

Caller: "Not today, but in the future...."

Me: "Tell you what, when you get your prototype built, send me a copy and let me test it for a week. I'll make a decision if it's something we'd be interested in and get back to you. Deal?"

Caller: "Uh, OK."

That call occurred six months ago. I still haven't received his "hardware-software" contraption. My point, however, is that I had to do a lot of fishing before I finally got to the truth. He didn't lie exactly. When I asked him a direct question, he answered it.

In contrast, it's the outright lies, misstatements of fact and half-truths that are really upsetting. This next story is a good example.

For several months, "IncompetentFolks.com" and "RighteousFolks.com" had worked together to develop an application for my company. From all indications, the project appeared to be going along smoothly. There were no signs of distress. Sure, there were the usual glitches here and there, but nothing out of the ordinary. My only red flag was that Righteous always blamed Incompetent for the problems.

Prior to launching the application, I asked both firms to participate in a live proof-of-concept demonstration at my office. The demo was to take place at 10 a.m. on a Friday, with both firms arriving the night before to set up and conduct a run-through. Because there would be several high-level individuals from Frederick Gold in attendance, I didn't want there to be any surprises.

This was one of those Important Meetings. My firm's executives wanted to see if we were getting our money's worth. I just wanted to see if the application actually worked before we released it to our customers.

At 4 p.m. on Thursday, the team from IncompetentFolks.com arrived in town and my administrative assistant lead them to the demo room. They were right on schedule. I had planned to join them shortly after I finished up another meeting.

At 4:30 p.m., my cell phone rang. It was Jacob Solomon, the president of RighteousFolks.com. Did I have a moment to talk, he wondered? I said yes and excused myself from the meeting. In the hallway, I listened as Jacob told me in a matter-of-fact voice that his company would not be participating in the demo tomorrow. The reason: IncompetentFolks.com and Jacob's company still had not signed a contract.

I was astounded. Here it was the night before and I was just learning of this situation. How could the two companies have worked together for months without a contract—and never once mention it to me?

Jacob said he had informed Incompetent a week earlier that if they did not sign the contract, Righteous wasn't coming to our offices for the demo. Apparently, Incompetent decided to call Jacob's bluff and chose not to sign.

In effect, RighteousFolks.com had used the demonstration—and my company—as ransom in an attempt to get a signed contract from IncompetentFolks.com. This ranked among the lowest of the low.

Up to this point, I thought Jacob and I had an honest and open working relationship. I trusted what he said and generally found his personnel to be more proficient than the employees at IncompetentFolks.com. This latest turn of events, however, caused me to question my relationship with Jacob.

Why, I asked, was he just now telling me this news? Did he want me to intervene? Was this just a courtesy call? What, exactly, did he want from me?

If I could intervene, that would be great, he told me. According to him, he was merely phoning to give me a "heads-up" so that we "wouldn't be caught off-guard" the next morning when his representatives didn't arrive. With nothing else to say, I ended the call and returned to my meeting.

For the next two hours, I sat and stewed. As important as this new development was, I couldn't walk out of my current meeting.

At 6:30 that evening, I went upstairs to the room where IncompetentFolks.com was setting up. I introduced myself to everyone and took in the sight. The room was a complete mess. Cable was strung all over. Monitors and laptops were everywhere. Boxes, Styrofoam and suitcases obscured the floor and tabletops. About the only thing missing was the Righteous team and their contribution to the hardware strewn about.

Everyone was breaking a sweat. Everyone, that is, except Lou Lipski, Incompetent's Vice President. He apparently didn't want to soil his perfectly starched designer shirt.

"Where are the folks from Righteous?" I inquired.

"They're coming at 6 p.m." Lou replied, grinning at me.

I looked at the clock on the wall. Actually, there were three clocks on the wall: One for local time, one for Europe and one for Asia. The local clock clearly read 6:30 p.m.

"It's 6:30 now, isn't it?"

"Not in California!"

Lou's flippant response sent his colleagues into a fit of laughter. Apparently, I was the only person who didn't appreciate the humor.

"Has anyone called them?"

"No. They'll be here. They're probably just stuck in traffic."

I could see this was going nowhere. I told them I'd be back in a moment. I left and went down the hall to a conference room. Once inside, I placed a call to Jacob Solomon's cell phone. The background noise clearly indicated he was in an airport terminal.

"Jacob, is there any possible way IncompetentFolks.com could still think you're coming tonight at 6 p.m.?"

"None. We told their people yesterday when we were rehearsing our presentation that we weren't showing if the contract wasn't signed."

"Give me five minutes. I'll call you back."

I hung up and went back down the hall to where Incompetent was setting up. When I opened the door, they were still laughing.

"May I see you outside for a moment?" I said to Lou, motioning for him to join me. At that point, the laughter started to fade and quick glances were exchanged among his team. Once outside, I told Lou that I was concerned Righteous had not arrived. This wasn't like them, I said. They were always quite punctual to appointments.

I suggested that we go down the hall and call them. As we walked to the conference room, I asked Lou if there was any reason that he knew of why Righteous wasn't here.

"None."

"Do you have a signed contract with them?"

"Yes. The contract was signed a long time ago."

I said nothing. A moment later, we arrived at the conference room, entered and closed the door. I dialed the phone. Jacob answered on the first ring. I activated speaker feature on my phone.

"Jacob," I said, "I'm here with Lou Lipski, who's vice president of IncompententFolks.com."

"Hi, Lou," said Jacob. "I've met lots of people from IncompetentFolks.com but not you."

"Well it's good to finally talk now. Where's your team?"

"Lou, my team's not coming. We made it very clear to your folks yesterday that unless we had a signed contract, we wouldn't come."

I looked at Lou for his reaction. His face was turning red and his hands actually began to tremble. Several seconds passed. Lou never met my gaze, but instead continued to focus on the phone.

"…This is the first I've heard about this…"

"I don't know what to say, Lou. We've been very clear with your people. It seems your attorney can't find the time to review the document we delivered to him several days ago."

Lou, a former consultant, was doing his best to keep his cool. His voice, however, was beginning to quaver.

"This is unfair to us—and to the client. It's a very unreasonable thing you're doing."

"I don't want to do this and I don't want to jeopardize my company's relationship with Frederick Gold, Inc., but enough is enough."

At this point, there were sounds of shuffling coming through the phone and a woman's voice saying "We've got to go—*now*."

"Look Lou, the ground crew is telling me that if I don't get onboard, I'm going to miss my flight."

"Alright, can you send me a copy of the contract?

"I'll e-mail it to you when I land. Tell me your address."

Lou provided the information and a moment later the call concluded. He then turned to me. It was the first time he had looked me in the eye since I asked him if the contract was signed.

"Well," said Lou, "I'm going to need a little assistance from you."

The man had no shame.

"I'm sorry," I told him, "but I'm going home now. You and Righteous will have to work this one out on your own. Call me when you resolve your issues." With that, I turned and walked away.

Lou trailed after me to the elevator, babbling on about how everything would be all right. "Don't worry," he said, "we've got plenty of time to work things out." As the elevator doors closed, the last thing I saw was the cheese-eating grin on his face. He was back to his usual self.

That evening, I was so upset I couldn't eat dinner. Once again, another eleventh-hour stunt by an Internet company was going to put a project in jeopardy. For several hours, I literally paced around my house, unable to concentrate. Around 10 p.m., my cell phone rang. It was Lou.

"We've worked it out. RighteousFolks.com is coming tomorrow, so you can sleep easy. By the way, we didn't know about the contract threat until yesterday at 3 p.m."

This was a revelation. When did Righteous actually issue its threat? Was it "a week ago," as Jacob Solomon had told me, or "yesterday at 3 p.m.," as Lou claimed? Further, did Lou, a vice president, really not know about the contract situation or did he know but instead choose to lie?

I don't know. In fact, when Lou and I ended this most recent call, it was still unclear whether a contract between the two parties had been signed. I didn't really care as long as the Righteous team arrived.

I didn't sleep that night. In fact, I was on the verge of being physically sick. After waiting months for the project to be delivered and then to have this sort of behavior occur was beyond unacceptable.

The next morning, it took all I had to get myself out of bed, showered and ready for work. Once at the office, I distracted myself with other tasks until 10 a.m. came. I didn't want to visit the room where the demo would take place for fear of what I might find.

At the appointed hour, I made my way upstairs. When I reached the conference room, I stood with my hand on the doorknob wondering what would await me on the other side.

"Are you going in or aren't you?" a voice said from behind me.

I turned around. It was Russell Dunn, our ever-jovial chief technology officer.

"You've been standing there for the last twenty seconds. Got a lot on your mind, do you?" he joked.

"Something like that," I said.

With Russell at my side, I swung open the door and entered. To my surprise, the room looked much different than the night before. In place of the boxes and packing material were fifteen well-dressed individuals seated around the conference table.

I immediately recognized the executives from my company and the folks from IncompetentFolks.com. But where was RighteousFolks.com? I now looked around the room a second time and still didn't see them. As the door swung closed, I turned and saw two people—the RighteousFolks.com representatives—standing behind the door. They smiled at me and laughed a little. I must have looked terrified. I smiled back and tried to appear calm.

Despite the events of the last sixteen hours, the show would go on.

In a way, it was almost anti-climactic. Although the product had some glitches, it worked. Afterward, I clenched my teeth and thanked everyone for their participation. I excused myself and got something to eat. It was the first food I could stomach since lunch the day before.

The demo may have been uneventful, but I was still fuming. I learned later that afternoon that a contract between the two companies had not been signed. Rather, RighteousFolks.com was compelled to attend because of some reverse threats by IncompetentFolks.com. The whole ordeal was sickening.

That afternoon, I couldn't get any work done. I hadn't been this miserable in years. I left work early that Friday, but not before sending an e-mail to the CEOs and other key persons at both IncompetentFolks.com and RighteousFolks.com. The wording was strong: Behavior of the sort exhibited by both firms over the last day would not be tolerated. This was not the way I conducted business nor was it the way in which my company had conducted business over the last century.

After I sent the e-mail, I felt better—for about five minutes. The whole event again reminded me of my time in the film industry and why I had left. I absolutely hated the duplicity and petty gamesmanship. Over the weekend, I seriously considered resigning my position. I wanted nothing to do with those damn dot-coms and the way they handled themselves.

Why do people at companies like IncompetentFolks.com and RighteousFolks.com engage in the behaviors and business practices that they do? Is it because they're evil? Some are, of course. But the real answer, I think, is that whether they're honest or intentionally dishonest, all Internet firms realize how tenuous their situation is. They're perpetually one step ahead of catastrophe.

If the founders of a dot-com can just keep the hype going long enough and get a few big-name people or companies to buy in—and bring credibility to the fledgling enterprise—they can reach the Promised Land. For a dot-com, this means the Initial Public Offering.

Chapter 19
The End Game

In the Old Economy, taking a company public meant that you were offering investors the opportunity to participate in a profitable venture. In fact, it was pretty much a requirement that a company had to make money before most respectable investment banking firms would even touch the prospectus.

Today, the Initial Public Offering (IPO) has degenerated into little more than a financing scam designed to let the entrepreneurs, venture capital firms and investment bankers cash out and leave some poor schmo in Des Moines holding worthless stock.

Sound harsh? Take a gander at the stock charts for most dot-coms and look at what's happened since they went public. Consider the following stocks:

	Opening Day*	High	Oct 23, 2000
Stamps.com	$15	$98.5	$2 25/32
US Interactive	$10	$92	$1 13/52
Ventro	$40	$243.5	$5 13/16
WebVan Group	$25	$34	$1 1/16

*Note: Opening Day amounts are within $5.

If that doesn't prove the point, check out the Internet message boards for various New Economy firms. Here, you'll discover the lamentations of people who bought at $18 per share—or higher—and have seen their investment dwindle to $1.50 per share, where it's been stagnating for the last twelve months.

Here's an appalling fact: Most dot-coms that go public have *never* made an operating profit. Not even a penny. Nothing. Not in their entire existence. In fact, they aren't expected to make a profit for years, if at all. So why would anyone invest in them? As someone once said, "there's a sucker born every minute."

Let's be clear: In most instances, one is not "investing" when it comes to dot-coms, but rather "gambling" on mythical future performance. After all, who wants to get left out of the New Economy?

Have you ever read the prospectus for an IPO? Most people haven't. The language is complex. The print is tiny. Besides, why let the details get in the way of a good story.

I'm convinced that the majority of investors, if they actually read—and understood—the prospectus, would never buy shares of an Internet firm.

Here's a good example: On one of my many airplane trips, I reached into the seat pocket to pull out the in-flight magazine. Instead, I found myself holding a draft prospectus for a forthcoming IPO. Apparently, the last passenger had forgotten to take it with him. So here I was reading it—which is exactly why I got so upset with the consulting firm for leaving my confidential binder in the taxi. You never know who's going to get their hands on your information.

The prospectus was typical in many respects. It contained several pages of risk factors, which alone should give most investors pause. Additionally, it noted that the dot-com had sustained substantial losses during its brief operating history. Again, nothing out of the ordinary. What really caught my attention, however, was the description under the section: "Use of Proceeds." Here's what it said:

"The primary purpose of this offering is to take advantage of favorable market conditions to raise additional equity capital, create a public market for our common stock and facilitate future access to public markets. *We have no current specific plans for the net proceeds from this offering.*" [italics added]

This is a company that's losing millions of dollars and is saying, essentially, "Give us your money. We're not sure what we'll do with it, but you can trust us to spend it wisely." Would you give a company like this your hard-earned cash? Surprisingly, many people did. A few months later, after the IPO, I did some research and discovered that the company, which I'll call "The Stiletto Group, Inc.," raised almost $40 million. The shares were priced around $10 and held steady the first day.

In the months following the IPO, however, it was the same old story. The stock was bid up and up—to over $80 per share. Then came the inevitable decline. In this case right back to $10. Between June of '00 and February '01, the stock was trading between $10 and $20. A quick check of the Internet message boards finds the typical postings from disgruntled shareholders.

There's an attitude in the United States that "everyone's getting rich but me." It's distorted thinking, fueled by magazine cover stories and primetime news programs that show the conspicuous consumption of a select few individuals in the New Economy.

In reality, the wealth stratification in Silicon Valley is much the same as it is in Hollywood. There are a few obscenely rich individuals who garner lots of publicity. However, for every millionaire, there are hundreds of people scraping by on $35,000 or less. Just as we worship actors and actresses, so do we worship the few New Economy moguls who have managed to strike it rich.

So, how does one prosper in the New Economy without losing her shirt? Surprisingly, by following some of the same principles that lead to success in the Old Economy.

SECTION FOUR:
EVERYTHING OLD IS NEW AGAIN

CHAPTER 20
THE RINGLEADERS

Of all the groups trying to make money by hyping the New Economy, there's one that's particularly repugnant. The consultants. They've played an integral role in creating hysteria among Old Economy firms. In fact, they've been at ground zero of the "you just don't get it" campaign.

Here's a dirty little secret: Consultants don't understand the New Economy. No kidding. They're as clueless as the rest of us. But, being consultants, they love to create client (and potential client) angst whenever there's any sort of uncertainty.

As mentioned previously, virtually every call I take from consultants promises me The Answer for success in the New Economy. However, they always want to know my e-commerce strategy prior to sharing their wisdom. Whatever you do, don't fall for this trick.

If consultants claim to have The Answer, then let them tell you. They don't need to know your strategy beforehand.

Why do consultants play this little game? Because they don't have an answer. They're hoping you'll tell them something that, along with everything else they've learned from calling others, will lead them in the right direction. Refuse to play along.

After speaking with several consultants, I realized they could be grouped into two broad categories. The first consists of well-known Old Economy consulting firms that now profess to understand the New

Economy. The other category consists of Web page design start-ups that claim to "do it all—from start to finish."

Regardless of the category, consultants want relationships with Old Economy firms for two reasons: Money and Credibility.

Sound familiar? It should. These are the same reasons that most Internet-related firms want to partner with Old Economy companies. In fact, the behaviors and words of e-commerce consultants are quite similar to that of dot-coms.

Here's an example of how the typical e-commerce consultant works. Remember Preacher Man from Chapter One? He was the self-proclaimed "leading New Economy expert" who proselytized about the Internet to a standing-room-only audience of Frederick Gold employees. Guess what? He's actually on the faculty of a reputable business school.

As you may recall, Preacher Man—a.k.a. "Professor Martinez"—delivered a message of fear in which he said, essentially, "if you don't do as I say, you won't know what hit you." A key part of his presentation was that "information aggregation sites" on the Internet would displace us from our customers. These sites would become The Source for unbiased, respected information on specific topics, such as outpatient health care. According to the professor, these sites would be the "*Consumer Reports* of the Internet."

Of course, the key flaw in Dr. Martinez's theory was that all the sites he used as examples accepted advertising and sponsorship money. *Consumer Reports* does not, which is exactly why it is respected for its unbiased ratings.

Minutes after his presentation, Martinez met with our vice president of corporate strategy behind closed doors.

If Dr. Martinez's objective was to create anxiety in our organization, it worked liked a charm. For two weeks, everyone ran around proclaiming that we were doomed.

Just when the hysteria was reaching its peak, our corporate strategy VP received a well-timed call from Dr. Martinez. "Would you be interested in a solution to the problem?" Dr. Martinez casually inquired. Let it be duly noted that our firm faced no problem until the arrival of the good professor.

What was our VP to say? He was getting deluged from all sides. He certainly didn't want to be the one responsible for bringing down a century-old company if there was an answer at hand. "Of course," he told Martinez, "we would most definitely be interested."

So it was that I got the assignment of following up with Dr. Martinez. When I called him, he immediately referred me to a particular dot-com.

It turned out Martinez's "solution" was actually the dot-com's Web site. This start-up company claimed to have designed a proprietary way of collecting and presenting information on health care topics so that a person could start their research at, say, a fourth grade reading level and then progress all the way up to what physicians were reading in their journals.

It wasn't a tricky concept to grasp, but it took me well over twenty minutes of questioning to cut through the babble.

I asked for the URL and visited the site myself. It was a huge disappointment. Essentially, all the "proprietary software" did was serve as a search engine. This was nothing new at all. Yahoo! and others have been doing it for years. Worse, unlike Yahoo!, the visitor would not be taken directly to the site they had searched for. Rather, this site would be "framed" within the dot-com's site, so that it appeared the dot-com was the source of information. Lastly, there was no rhyme or reason to the manner in which the searched articles were presented. It was a scam of the highest degree.

When I asked about the segmentation of research by reading level, going from low to high, I was told it was forthcoming. Dr. Martinez's solution was quickly unraveling.

What the dot-com really wanted from us was money so my company's information would receive preferential treatment when the search results were listed. In essence, my firm's content would be pushed to the top of the list. This went against everything Dr. Martinez stated in his presentation about unbiased information.

But the biggest surprise of all was still to come. It turned out that Dr. Martinez had a board seat with this dot-com. As such he had a vested interest in steering business to it. In all likelihood, the dream was that one day the dot-com would go public and everyone would be rich, including Dr. Martinez.

I've asked many people the following question: "Did Dr. Martinez have an obligation to reveal that he was on the board when he proposed the dot-com firm as a solution?" The answers vary. To me, the conflict of interest is clear. Eventually, Martinez came clean—but only at the last minute as I was conducting my due diligence effort.

Let's take a moment to recap the above situation. A well-known professor/consultant at a top business school visits an Old Economy firm and creates a problem where none existed. Near-hysteria ensues. The consultant then miraculously offers a solution. The solution doesn't live up to its hype. The consultant is found to have a vested interested in the proposed solution.

The moral of this story is that many e-commerce consultants—including, unfortunately, some "well-respected academics"—will try to make a buck off the Internet through nothing but sheer hype.

Let's continue to build on this issue, because, to a large extent, the evolution of the Internet has been driven by hype coming from the mouths of consultants. At first, consultants proclaimed that all companies should have a Web site. You were dead if you didn't have one, they said. Hence, consultants made a lot of money getting everyone to establish a presence on the Internet.

Why did companies need to have a Web site? To interact with their customers, according to the consultants. This was known as B2C, or

Business-to-Consumer. Of course, it takes more than just a primitive "brochure-ware" Web site to interact with one's customers.

Web sites are hungry beasts. In most instances, they need to have fresh and/or compelling content placed on them frequently to entice visitors to return time and time again.

It soon became painfully clear to consultants that this would require more work than initially thought. And the payoff was anything but certain. There were, after all, few examples of good B2C Web sites that drew large amounts of repeat visitor traffic—and profits.

What to do? Forget B2C. It was so old-fashioned anyway. Begin promulgating Business-to-Business. B2B was really where it was at, the consultants said. Of course, the consultants had been shrewd. B2B is generally not glamorous. It consists of mundane, back-office operations such as billing—exactly the type of repetitive activities that computers can do well.

In contrast, B2C is fairly sexy in that for almost next to nothing (excluding the consulting fees) anyone can have a presence on the Internet. The issue with B2C, however, is that it's very difficult to generate a positive bottom line—something scores of dot-coms learn every day. By getting Corporate America to test the waters with B2C, the consultants were now in a much better position to pitch B2B. Look around. The strategy is paying off. Ask any consultant worth his salt and he'll recite the same mantra: "B2C is dead. Long live B2B."

What's next in the evolution of the New Economy? It's simple. Follow the money and the hype. E-Commerce will give way to "m-commerce." This is the latest buzzword from the consultants. It refers to mobile commerce, meaning commerce conducted using cell phones and other wireless devices that utilize something known as WAP ("wireless application protocol") and similar technologies.

It takes a lot of sustained hype to keep the New Economy humming along. Much of the mumbo-jumbo comes from a handful of consulting firms that claim to have their finger on the pulse of the New World.

These consulting firms play an integral role in driving the evolution of the New Economy. You're probably familiar with these companies. They spend a lot of time getting their name in the papers.

Like most people, I thought these firms knew what they were talking about. After all, they were cited in the *New York Times*, the *Wall Street Journal* and other well-respected publications. A few weeks into my job, I signed a year-long contract with one of the companies so I, too, wouldn't get left behind.

Shortly thereafter, the actual analyst reports started showing up. I was appalled. These consisted of little more than the regurgitation of press releases and sophomoric commentary. There was little true analysis.

In addition to the reports, our agreement entitled me to submit e-mail inquiries to the analysts. An example of such a request might be "which health care sites are visited most by women?" It was rare that the firm's responses directly addressed my questions. In fact, most times, I received non-answers.

After one of these run-arounds, I was angry enough to call my account rep directly. I got voice mail. So I started calling other people at the firm. There was no receptionist answering. It was voice mail wherever I went—and this included the president of the company. Keep in mind that this wasn't a holiday or a late Friday afternoon. It was the middle of the day on a Thursday. A few days later, I eventually got a return call from the president. He apologized and said he'd look into the situation. There was no company-wide staff meeting or anything like that. They simply weren't answering their phones.

Still another part of our service arrangement permitted me unlimited access to the firm's analysts. I didn't want to abuse the privilege, but I did want to have a monthly call. "No problem," I was promised. When I attempted to set up my first call, "unlimited" access began to have some restrictions associated with it. First, given the analysts' busy schedules, it would be very difficult to arrange a call. Second, if a call were arranged, I would have to submit a set of written questions several days prior. It was as though I was scheduling an interview with a celebrity.

To a certain extent, the analysts did view themselves as celebrities. There wasn't a day that went by when their names didn't appear in top publications. They were always ready with a quote. It was a little strange, however, that the research reports I actually received never contained the supporting material for what I read in the newspapers.

In fact, New Economy consulting firms share a great deal in common with the dot-coms. For both, selling the sizzle seems more important than delivering the product or service. In the case of the consulting firms, they often direct much of their attention to the media and little of it to the paying clients. It's another example of the tail wagging the dog.

One day I came across an interesting story from an online publication that referenced several of the New Economy consulting firms, including the one we contracted with. The story was quite harsh and implied that the firms really didn't have a grasp of what was going on. Rather, the story said, it was just a bunch of precocious twenty-something adults struggling to keep the hype going. Sadly, I had to admit that this had been my experience.

One ominous sign that my e-commerce consulting firm was facing difficulties came when its IPO was delayed. Apparently, the company was going through tough times. This was reflected in how my reports were delivered to me. When I first started receiving the analysts' papers, they came three-hole punched and were to be placed into glossy binders supplied by the consulting firm. Now, the reports started showing up un-punched. I asked why. It turned out they were going to a new "storage system methodology" that consisted of "lovely" plastic boxes. I asked where my boxes were. They'd be at my desk "any day now" I was told.

A few weeks later, the boxes did arrive. They were cheap and barely stood up when assembled. It was obvious that the consulting firm, like so many Internet companies before it, had been living too high on the hog and was now looking to cut back on expenses. Strangely, they chose to pinch pennies on supplying their paying customers with binders rather than through other cost-cutting measures, such as moving to less expensive office space.

During the twelve months of our contract, I spoke with the consultants several times about the quality of their offering. It never did improve. Ironically, they would seek customer feedback fairly often. At each opportunity, I would convey my dissatisfaction. In turn, they promised to do better. They never did.

When it came time to renew, they appeared truly shocked that I cancelled our subscription. They listed every excuse in the book about why they had been unable to deliver. All their problems seemed to be quite Old Economy in nature, which was puzzling given that they were such advocates of how the New Economy would change everything.

The bottom line is this: You know just as much as the Internet consultants at this point—and probably more—when it comes to your company and the New Economy. Honest. Sure, you could pay lots of money to learn this the hard way, like my firm did, but why?

Here's what you should do instead. Forget the consultants. Rather, make the effort to build the competency *within* your organization to understand the New Economy. After all, you're going to need this capability in the future. Why not start building it now? The next chapter outlines some concrete suggestions.

CHAPTER 21
TEN LESSONS FROM THE FRONT LINE

When my one-year anniversary arrived on August 8, 2000, I took a few moments to reflect upon what had transpired over the last twelve months.

Our group was still in place—none of us had been fired or had left the company to join a dot-com. In fact, we had expanded by several more people. That was a good sign.

The vendor phone calls were still coming, although they had diminished a little in volume after the April 2000 stock market "correction." The calls from consultants wanting to provide us with The Answer continued unabated as well. On a positive note, the more sophisticated callers were no longer using the "I'll show you mine if you show me yours" tactic of asking for our Internet strategy before stating what they had to offer.

As for the projects I had worked on, there wasn't much good news to report. Sure, I'd saved the company millions of dollars by not pursuing some horrible deals like the one offered by Outpatient-clinic.com. But I hadn't made the company any money, either.

The enormously expensive sponsorship deal with Hypemeister.com had yielded few measurable results. The Vaporcon pilot missed one deadline after another. Six months after we signed the contract, it still wasn't running. Additionally, there were several other potential deals we pursued. They all sounded good initially, but eventually wound up as dead ends.

Without a doubt, the past year has been both the most exciting and stressful of my life. I had an unbelievable opportunity to see first-hand what really goes on behind the scenes of the so-called New Economy. As you know now, it's even more absurd than what you read in the newspapers and see on TV.

Over the last twelve months, I did indeed "work harder," just as Maxine Lancaster said when she offered me the job. In fact, my social life never really did improve and neither did my bouts of insomnia. Still, I wouldn't trade the opportunity I was given. I learned a tremendous amount in my assignment. By the end of my year, I'd like to think that I was not only working harder, but also smarter.

The Internet, e-commerce and the New Economy aren't mystical. And they shouldn't be. If a few basic principles are followed, virtually any Old Economy company can prosper in the New Economy. I've compiled a list of lessons learned that many Old Economy companies—large or small—will find useful as they venture forth into the New Economy and find themselves face-to-face with the characters that populate it.

Of course, I can't guarantee success—after all, I'm not a consultant. However, I can confidently say that you'll have a much better chance of securing competitive advantage and, hence, of being successful if you consider the following Lessons.

By the way, none of this is rocket science. It's just the unglamorous basics. Old Economy stuff. Surprisingly though, it works.

1. Establishing Your e-Commerce Effort: Securing Buy-In

What type of organization do you have, Democracy or Dictatorship? The answer will determine how you go about starting or modifying your e-commerce effort. As you saw earlier in the first few chapters, my company is a democracy. Building consensus is incredibly important. Telling people what they're going to do generally doesn't work. They have to understand why they're being asked to do something and how it will benefit them.

Even if your company tends to be more of a dictatorship, you'll find yourself pushing rope uphill if it's not clear why you're establishing an e-commerce group. One of the first questions you'll get is, "What's our e-commerce strategy?" If your people don't like the answer or feel that key individuals weren't involved in formulating it, you'll face a long, arduous task to get their support.

Remember what happened to my firm when several key people were invited ostensibly to participate in the development of the strategy only to find a strategy had already been developed? We lost valuable months trying to smooth over hurt feelings. Some people still weren't on board—twelve months later.

Every organization is full of politics. Most likely, yours is no different. It's critical that the key constituents in your company are invited early on to an open discussion about what you endeavor to achieve regarding e-commerce. Almost certainly, not everyone will agree. But if they feel they've been heard and their ideas were considered, you'll find yourself in a much better position two months down the road.

Yes, I know the above concept sounds painfully simple. However, it's surprising how many times organizations charge forward under the false assumption that buy-in has occurred only to learn later that it hasn't. Do yourself a favor and take a little extra time up front to make sure the key people in your company understand why you're embarking on an e-commerce effort. It's important enough to consider a one-or two-day off-site meeting away from phones, voicemail and other office distractions.

2. Staffing Your e-Commerce Team

Who do you want on your e-commerce team? Here's a list of characteristics:

- Outstanding business judgment
- Enjoy (or at least tolerate) ambiguity
- Deep knowledge of your business and the environment in which it operates
- Objective thought process
- Curious/Willing to learn
- Well-networked inside and outside your organization
- Well-respected within your organization
- Demonstrated project management and negotiation skills
- Willingness to take sensible risk [Note: this does not mean reckless behavior]
- Team players with a past track record of success in a variety of assignments

Look around your organization. How many people have the above characteristics? It may be fewer than you think. Getting the right people on your team is essential. They'll set the level of performance, which will determine who joins the group later when it expands. You don't want to populate the group with just any warm bodies. It's too important.

You may ask, is "e-commerce experience" necessary for your team members? My answer is that it's preferred for some but by no means a requirement for all. A familiarity with the Internet, however, is something you'll want every member of your team to have.

By far, however, the most important attribute you want from your e-commerce people is strong business judgment. They'll be asked to trudge through a lot of manure. You want people who can think things through and not get caught up in the hype.

3. Governance and Organizational Structure

Regarding organizational structure, one thing my firm did especially well was to place the e-commerce group in our marketing department. Although the team has strong links to our various IT components, I wouldn't recommend putting your e-commerce group under the IT function. This isn't to say that IT is inferior to marketing. It's not. You're just looking for a different skill set.

Your e-commerce team should be cross-functional. You'll need to have at least one attorney on board. Ideally, this is a lawyer who not only knows your business inside and out but also thoroughly understands technology and intellectual property issues. If this person doesn't exist in your organization, pay big bucks to bring one in from outside. You need an attorney with the above capabilities. Don't skimp on this one. I couldn't do what I do without the close participation of skilled e-commerce attorneys.

You'll also need strong ties to your business development folks. These are people who conduct the serious due diligence necessary in dealing with dot-coms and other firms in the New Economy. You want people with top-notch financial skills, folks who can dissect a prospectus and the various financial statements to uncover the red flags. We're fortunate at our company to have an outstanding business development group, which makes my job infinitely easier.

Of course, the individuals on your core e-commerce team should have the skills mentioned in the previous section. These people are your workhorses. They'll do your environmental assessment (see next sec-

tion), match your business needs with appropriate opportunities, negotiate and oversee your pilot programs.

How many people will you need? That depends on your objectives.
We started with seven. Whatever you decide, I'd recommend starting
with a small number. You can always add additional team members
when needed.

With all these different groups—IT, legal, business development,
etc.—working so closely with one another and others in your organization, there are bound to be disagreements. As such, you'll need a system
to settle disputes. The consultants call this a "governance strategy." I call
it the Supreme Court.

Here's how it works. A group of three to five mutually agreed upon
"judges" is appointed. These folks are senior-level people at your firm
who have oversight responsibility for your e-commerce activities. When
disputes arise, the various parties involved first try to settle the issue
themselves. If they cannot, they ask to convene a special meeting of The
Court. Because the judges are busy individuals, requesting such a meeting should not be taken lightly.

When the court is in session, a representative from each of the dis-
puting parties presents his case. The judges deliberate and reach a decision. All decisions are final. Of course, if the judges feel the case is
without merit, they are free to reprimand one or both parties for wast-
ing their time. In this way, the parties are encouraged to work out disputes amongst themselves. Try it. You'll be pleasantly surprised just how
effective it is.

4. Environmental Assessment Competency

If you're serious about your e-commerce effort, you'll need to establish
an environmental assessment competency within your e-commerce
group. This means you need *at least* one individual who tracks the general

environment of your industry. By this, I mean all the goings-on of your competitors and the various constituents that directly or indirectly impact how you conduct business—both in the online and offline world.

The importance of building a competency in environmental assessment can't be stressed enough. Without it, your firm will find itself at the mercy of the consultants and New Economy companies. Every opportunity presented to you will sound fabulous. Before you know it, you won't know which way is up—which is exactly where they want you.

Don't let this happen. If you do, you'll find yourself *reacting* to every little event in the environment. Unfortunately, this is where many companies (and people) spend most of their time. It's dangerous. When you finally figure out what's happening, it's too late.

See if this example sounds familiar. A story appears on the front page of the *Wall Street Journal.* The article mentions a firm doing something that's tangentially related to your company and the way it conducts business. I'm willing to bet that within hours, there's a barrage of phone calls going back and forth between people at your organization asking, "Why aren't we doing that?" A few days later, money and other resources are being expended to see how your firm can do what the company in the article is doing—regardless of whether it's really in your firm's best interest to do so.

Imagine multiplying this scenario out several times over the course of a year. This is a classic example of a reactive company. Wouldn't it be better if, instead, you had a team at your firm that you could call and ask, "What do you make of the story in today's *Journal?*" Given the team's ongoing analysis, they can put the story in proper perspective and provide you with a recommendation.

Take the time to understand what's going on around you. Doing so will enable you to be proactive in your decision making. If you heed just one of the lessons in this section, let it be this one. By making proactive decisions based upon a sound, ongoing analysis of your competitive environment, your company will achieve an advantage over your competition.

Here's another benefit of environmental analysis: It enables one to differentiate fads from trends. If you're a teenager (or a company that caters to teenagers), going from fad to fad is great. For nearly everyone else, it's better to focus on trend identification.

Fads tend to come out of nowhere, peak quickly and then vanish without a trace. In fact, a graph of a fad tends to look like an upside down "V." See the illustration below.

In contrast, trends take a longer time to develop and are hard to identify without constant, ongoing analysis. Often, the upward slope of a trend line is quite gradual. At some point, however, when the time is right, the line shifts upward with a dramatically steeper slope. The trick is having the insight to gauge where in the "hockey stick" part of the curve the trend is and what factors will cause the line to shift upward. It's not easy, but doing the grunt work of environmental analysis will enable your firm to proactively place its bets in anticipation of the trend taking off.

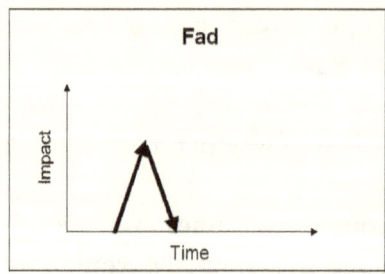 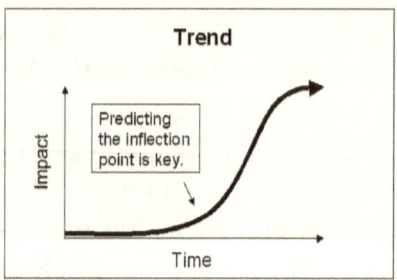

Sure, you say, environmental analysis works in the Old Economy where things move slowly. But it won't work in the New Economy where we move in Internet time. Well, I contend that most of what we've seen so far in the New Economy is nothing more than skipping from fad to fad—B2C, B2B, m-commerce, etc. Of course, underlying all the fads is a series of trends, such as increased usage of the Internet.

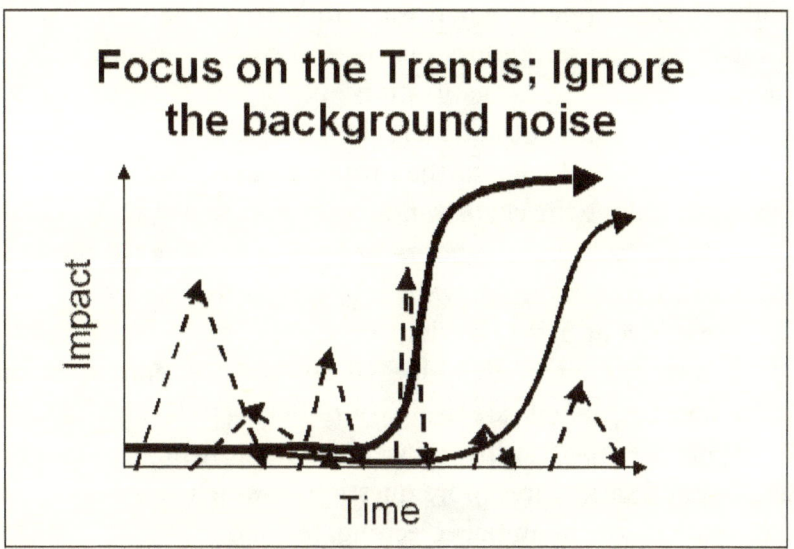

It's the proactive company that takes the time to identify and track these trends so they can best position themselves for the future.

Yes, the world is moving faster today. But people were saying the same thing a hundred years ago. The companies that are still thriving today are those that took the time to understand their competitive environment (and their customers) and adapted themselves as appropriate to the underlying trends, while diligently avoiding the fads.

5. Screening Vendors

At the same time you're conducting your environmental analysis, you'll also have to respond to the hundreds of New Economy vendors that call your firm. Unless you put adequate controls in place, you'll feel like your company is enduring a roach infestation.

As mentioned earlier, I'd strongly advocate that all calls dealing with e-commerce and the Internet go through a limited number of individuals. Additionally, you'll want to keep a database of all contacts made with these vendors that is read-only accessible by appropriate members of your organization outside the e-commerce team. In this way, everyone knows of previous conversations, and the vendor can be redirected back to the proper contact. Such a system will dramatically reduce the chaos vendors try to create at your company.

How should calls from vendors be screened? Here's a simple, but effective solution. Ask the following four questions:

1. What is your firm's offering?
2. Is your offering in use today? (If not, consider ending the call.)
3. How many people are using your offering today?
4. What is it, specifically, you want from our firm?

Sure, you can ask scores more questions—which you'll do if there's an interest. But for the initial screening, the above four will work just fine. You may even ask the vendor to submit additional documentation electronically so you can keep it along with your contact sheet. Surprisingly, many New Economy companies are not able to send electronic documentation, preferring instead to send hardcopy. I usually end these calls shortly thereafter. No one has time for a company that claims to be New Economy and yet does not have the capability to send documents electronically.

The key document in your vendor database is the Vendor Contact Sheet. You'll want to include these items on the sheet:

*   Company name
*   Contact name (and phone number, e-mail address, etc.)
*   Company phone number and address
*   Answers to the Four Questions
*   Any additional information that you deem relevant
*   A reverse chronological listing of all contacts with the vendor (date, time, who spoke with whom and what was discussed)

Here's an example:

> **Vendor Contact Sheet**
> ClinicKiosk.com
> Contact: Brad Spinman, Director of Business Development
> 123 Menlo Drive
> Alto Palo, MN 12345
> 650-650-1212
>
> Answers to Four Questions:
> Company is offering an Internet-linked computer kiosk for clinics.
> The kiosk is up and running today, although with limited functionality.
> They claim to have the kiosks installed in 1,000 clinics today
> throughout the country.
> They want us to sponsor certain topics on the kiosk.

Vendor Contact Sheet (Continued)

Call log:
08/01/00: Brad called again to see if I'd done my on-site visit. Told him I hadn't and to stop calling.
07/22/00: Brad called to see if I'd done my on-site visit. Told him I hadn't.
07/15/00: Brad called to schedule an on-site visit. Told him I'd look into it. Offers free trial.
07/06/00: Learn from Mary in US division that Brad is calling the brand teams about his kiosks. Place call to CEO of Brad's company. We discuss issue. Next step: He's to send location list to me. He does. Only 278 clinics verified. Not 500, as previously stated. Bad feeling about these folks. No more contact planned until I visit a couple of these clinics on my next trip out of town. No hurry on this one.
06/11/00: Brad comes to visit. Explains device. Interesting concept but I don't think patients will use it. Again ask him for list of locations. Apologizes for not sending it earlier and promises to send to me. Tells me he's got one of our competitors who will take this opportunity in next two weeks if we don't. I tell him not to wait for me. Next step: Visit some of these clinics and see first-hand if people are using the device.
05/11/00: Speak with Brad. He tells me they have 500 kiosks installed. (He's loose with his numbers.) Bottom line: Don't think this will work based on what he's telling me. Next step: Invite him in for a one-hour presentation on 6/11/00. Asked for listing of locations where kiosks are installed. Says he'll e-mail to me.
05/08/00: Brad Spinmeister calls Gerald Hogan and tells him about sponsorship opportunity on his company's Net kiosks in 1,000 doctor's offices. Gerald forwards to me for follow up.

As you know from earlier sections of the book, such a detailed vendor database will save you a lot of time and aggravation by catching half-truths and other misstatements of fact.

6. Matching Your Needs with the Best Vendor

Once you've gotten a handle on your competitive environment and created a vendor database, you're in a position to match your business needs with the capabilities of the vendors whom you've screened.

Here's how it works. Let's say one of your brand teams wants to incorporate some new whiz-bang technology into their Web site so they can solicit customer feedback. All you have to do is search through your vendor database and contact those vendors who have a solution for your need. Your database enables you to make true apples-to-apples comparisons between the various vendors, so your search goes quickly.

In some instances, there won't be an exact match between your needs and the solutions currently offered by the vendors. No problem. Your database is such that you have enough information to know which vendors, given their capabilities, may have the resources and know-how necessary to custom design a product for you. Again, you're saving yourself a ton of time cold-calling around by focusing on those firms that have the best chance of matching your needs.

Now, instead of reacting to vendors' calls telling you what you need, you're telling them what it is you want. Isn't it great to be proactive?

7. Negotiating

Much of this book has been spent on the grim details of what occurs during negotiations. Here are some tips to make your vendor discussions go as smoothly as possible.

I encourage you to have at least one member of the negotiating team stay involved with the project through implementation, preferably in a project management role. Although some folks advocate separating the negotiating team from the implementation team, I'm strongly opposed. Given the dishonesty and staffing turnover at most Internet firms, you'll be doing yourself a big favor to retain continuity on your team as you progress through the relationship. Even if you've got a contract that's a hundred pages long, you need to know the intent behind the words. The only way I know to do this is by having at least one person participate in the negotiations and in the implementation.

At a minimum, you'll want to have a core negotiating team consisting of a member of your e-commerce staff, an attorney and a business development person. If you're at a smaller firm, then you'll need to have a Jack (or Jill) of all trades take care of this function. Better, I think, to have a few people involved to bounce ideas off one another.

8. Pilot Programs: The Smart Way to Learn

What sorts of projects are you going to pursue, large- or small-scale? Given the level of uncertainty surrounding e-commerce and the Internet, you may want to start small with pilot projects and then enlarge them if appropriate.

Small-scale pilot projects are better for a number of reasons. They're manageable and enable you to focus on the lessons learned, as opposed to dealing with recruitment and other size issues. The Vaporcon people wanted us to implement with over 500 physicians. I realized early on that we'd been spending more time recruiting doctors to participate rather than focusing on the application itself. Instead, we agreed to go with fewer than 50 offices.

Additionally, if small-scale projects don't work out, there's not too much downside risk. It's relatively easy to make adjustments if changes are needed. If it's successful, it's easy to roll out to a larger scale. Let me clarify, however, that you need to know up front what will happen at the end of the pilot. Specifically, what will trigger the go/no-go decision to proceed? If you do go forward, you need to have thought through the scalability issues. How, for instance, will you roll out the offering to a group ten times the size that participated in your pilot? Do you have the necessary resources? Does your vendor?

Lastly, a small-scale pilot enables you to oversee it with a great deal of granularity. You'll be able to ask questions like, "Why did this work with Customer X when Customer Y hated it?" Answers to these questions are easier to discern in a pilot program than in a large-scale roll out.

Be forewarned that almost every vendor is going to encourage you to go big right off the bat. No matter how enticing they make it sound, resist the urge to do so. If your pilot is successful, you'll have ample opportunity to scale it up quickly.

9. Structuring the Pilots to Maximize Your Learning

More vendors than I can count have come to me promising a "positive return on investment" if only my firm would use their offering. If you're looking to get a positive ROI from your pilot programs at this stage of the game, you may want to adjust your thinking. Note that by "positive ROI" I mean the definition for return on investment found in traditional business textbooks—i.e. if I spend $100 and I get back $110, then I have a 10% return on my investment.

Consultants and dot-coms have come up with incredibly tortured New Economy definitions for ROI. Use them if you want. I prefer, however, to use the one that's been around for the last couple millenniums.

Instead of worrying about ROI at this point, concern yourself with establishing a set of low-cost learnings that will enable you to discover what works and what doesn't. This is essentially what the Gemini and Apollo Space Programs were all about—except that they were quite expensive. The analogy, though, holds in that the ultimate goal was to get a man on the moon. Of course, one doesn't just establish this objective and then put a person on top of a rocket the next day and assume they'll be successful. It took the United States nearly a decade to achieve its goal—and that was with virtually unlimited financial resources and the best engineering talent in the world.

Some may disagree with me, but I believe that the same incremental approach holds true for learning one's way in the New Economy. For instance, you first have to get people to come to your Web site before it's reasonable to expect to sell anything on it. If you know what your ultimate objective is, you can then work back through the process and lay out the necessary steps to be achieved along the way. Your e-commerce pilot projects are an excellent way to validate these milestones.

Please don't misunderstand and assume that I'm advocating paralysis by analysis when I talk about an incremental approach. I'm not. But you do need to have a well thought out game plan in place ahead of time for each of your pilot projects. By the way, your vendors don't need to know your overall strategy. They just need to know their role and how it pertains to the specific job you are asking them to do.

At this point, the question of cost arises. How much should you pay for your pilots? My short answer is, "not nearly as much as vendors will want."

It's always fascinating when consulting firms tell me it's cheaper to get in on the ground floor. I wish it were. However, it seldom is. As you know from the Outpatient-clinic.com example, New Economy companies will generally start the negotiations at a ridiculously high price, just to see if you'll bite. Better for you to do your research, create a "what-if" valuation model and counter with a price that you think is fair. Don't be too concerned when the vendor gets all blustery. Remember: They need you more than you need them.

10. Moving from Pilot to Full-Scale Implementation

At the time this book was written, this final lesson was a work-in-progress for my company. As you've read, we had not moved beyond the pilot phase with any of our projects. That said, if your pilot project delivers the results you had hoped for, the next step is to scale it up. At this point, the ROI question does need to be addressed. Perhaps there was no way to make money when the project was in pilot phase, but it should be expected to show a positive return when you move to full-scale implementation.

Your ROI calculation will need to take into account all of the elements necessary to scale up. Internet firms are fond of saying that it doesn't cost any more to have 100,000 people using an application than it does to have 100 people on board. For them, that may be the case because their variable costs are virtually zero. For you, these costs may be significant.

Be careful to consider all the expenses associated with taking a project from small-scale pilot to full-scale implementation. Distribution, promotion, you name it—all will have to be taken into account. It's instructive to remember that very few high-tech companies and almost no dot-coms have made an operating profit. You don't want to join them. You won't, if you think things through and avoid the hysteria—both inside and outside your firm.

CHAPTER 22
LOOKING AHEAD

As your company moves forward to implement its e-commerce strategy, here are some brief thoughts on four relevant topics.

"Exclusivity" on the Internet

There is no such thing—and there shouldn't be. Capitalism is built on choice. Let's give consumers choice. Here's one way to do this: Expand the use of hotlinks on the Web.

In nearly every financial article that appears on the Internet today, the first time a company's name appears in the article it occurs as a hotlink. You've seen this. The name is in blue and underlined. If you click on it, you're immediately transported to the company's Web site for additional information. Why can't this be done with product names when they're mentioned in an article, provided a Web site exists for that product?

It's true that this occurs at some sites today—but generally because the company paid to have its product name hotlinked. "Open hotlinking" for products and services will only help to increase the time people spend online by making their information searches all that much easier.

Banner Ads and Sponsorship "Opportunities"

Banner ads have been a huge disappointment. A story in the September 1, 2000 *Wall Street Journal* noted that the click-through rate for banner ads is less than 0.5%—and declining. Some companies are paying less than $5 per 1,000 "impressions," or the number of times a banner appears on a particular Web page. The industry average is between $20 and $30 per 1,000 impressions—down significantly from a year before.

Why are banner ads such dogs? It has to do with finite vs. "infinite" ad space inventory. For instance, advertisers know that there are only about six minutes of ads during any 30-minute TV show. The ad space inventory is fixed.

Contrast this with the Net, where the possible ad space is virtually infinite. In essence, it's analogous to posting a handwritten sign for a garage sale on a telephone pole. We drive by hundreds of phone poles each day. So much so that we don't even notice them anymore, let alone something posted on them.

Banner ads are an attempt at "one-to-many" communication, which describes a TV commercial. However, as Seth Godin says in his book, *Permission Marketing*, the Internet is best used for one-to-one communication where the consumer permits you to discourse with him or her. Banner ads just don't deliver one-to-one.

Sponsorship opportunities are no better. It's clear to me what the value is to the company collecting my sponsorship money: They get my money *and* the credibility of being associated with my firm. In comparison, it's less clear what benefit my company gets out of the deal. All I see are the negatives, including dilution of my company's hard-earned reputation. Additionally, I risk putting a middleman between me and my customers.

Both banner ads and sponsorship opportunities are an attempt to impose a revenue model on the Internet that's worked for broadcast television and radio over the last 50 years. Shame on all of us associated with the Web if we allow this medium to become "Television II—a second Vast Wasteland."

Building the New Economy's Infrastructure

Who has the responsibility to build the e-infrastructure of Internet firms so they can achieve a critical mass of users? Is it the fledgling New Economy companies or the Old Economy companies who have money? To hear the vendors who call me every day, it's the Old Economy companies. But do profitable Old Economy firms really have what I call a "moral obligation" to provide the dot-coms with money—at zero interest—for their infrastructure needs?

I don't think so.

It would be like Ted Turner having asked my company—and not his financiers—to fund CNN when it was built. I'm happy to advertise on his network, but there's no way I'm going to build it. The same is true for dot-coms. Let the venture capital firms build the infrastructure and be appropriately rewarded for taking the risk.

Success and the New Economy

So what's the secret to long-term success in the New Economy?

I contend it is this: The ability to successfully implement your business strategy in a way that establishes trust and credibility with your customers.

Go back and read it a second time. Slowly. Essentially, it's the same Old Economy business principle that has been with us for thousands of years.

Let me provide an example. In the 1970s Toyota (and other Japanese car manufacturers), came across a great business strategy: Build an automobile with almost zero defects, that gets great gas mileage and is priced competitively. Were they able to successfully implement this strategy? Ask General Motors. Better yet, ask any Toyota owner. It's taken years for American carmakers to build vehicles of similar quality.

Toyota made a promise *and* delivered on it. Did the company successfully implement its strategy overnight? No. A lot of people toiled in anonymity for years to transform the idea into a reality. But the payoff was worth it.

In light of the above, what can we say about the New Economy? Certainly, it will bring many efficiencies and innovations to business in ways that we can only begin to imagine. At the end of the day, however, any enterprise that aspires to long-term success in this Brave New World will still have to employ basic business principles to build trust and credibility among its customers. Hype will not suffice.

Consider what transpired during Super Bowl XXXIV, which aired on January 30, 2000. Of the 40-plus advertisers, around half were New Economy businesses. What did these firms get in return for spending approximately $2 million per 30-second ad? Not much. It's now common knowledge that many of them experienced tough times in the months following the game. As of this writing, at least two of the firms—Epidemic.com and Pets.com—are now longer in business. Again, hype will not redeem a weak business plan.

Throughout the ages, there have been many "New Economies." Yet, the bedrock concept of profitability has not changed—despite what the consultants, entrepreneurs and other gurus might spew forth. Follow their siren call if you want. But the winners, I believe, will be those who apply rational business judgment to the myriad decisions facing them. They'll take sensible risk, learn quickly and strengthen their credibility with customers. And they'll do this while keeping close watch over the bottom line, thereby creating true value.

Ironically, one might say that everything old is new again.

EPILOGUE

How times change. When I started my e-commerce assignment in August 1999, many people in the New Economy kept telling me that I didn't "get it." Yet, it appears that I "got it" all along. Beyond the hype and hysteria, there simply wasn't much to get.

By March 2001, others were finally discovering this sad fact, too. In contrast to when I began my job, a handful of New Economy companies were now being *removed* from the Nasdaq each day. Vaporcon was one of these firms. Thank goodness we had terminated our agreement with them several months before. We also had the good fortune to end our relationship with IncompetentFolks.com and RighteousFolks.com before they came upon hard times.

For many people, 2001 stands in stark contrast to the way they had lived only a year before. Indeed, the number of unsolicited resumes that I receive from former dot-com employees has grown substantially in recent months. These people all tell me similar stories about how things "just didn't work out" in their New Economy jobs.

In spite of all this, there are still some in the New Economy who find it difficult to give up their addiction to hype. Here's a case in point.

At a recent business conference, there were two speakers. The first was from an Old Economy company. The title of his talk was, "How to Meld New Economy Ideas with Old Economy Discipline." The second speaker was from a well-known New Economy company—not a small dot-com start-up, but the sort of firm that's featured regularly in various business magazines. The title of his talk was, "E-Commerce: What's Real and What's Not."

The Old Economy CEO gave an excellent presentation. He spoke exactly on his topic. In contrast, the New Economy executive threw the audience a curve ball by deviating from his publicized topic. For the first thirty minutes, he talked about a pilot program where his company's equipment was being utilized. The remainder of his talk was a case study—using his company as the example—for how the New Economy changes the way we'll all do business. In essence, his presentation amounted to one long advertisement for his firm.

At the end of his talk, we were told the New Economy speaker had time for just one question. A member of the audience went quickly to a microphone.

"Your talk was entitled, 'E-Commerce: What's Real and What's Not.' Would you would take a moment here to address that topic?"

It was a great question. The speaker, a former consultant, had the following response:

"You're right, that *was* the title of my talk. But on the long plane ride here, I decided to speak on a different topic…."

The man's answer clearly illustrates the key point of this book. It all comes down to trust and credibility. Do you keep your promise with the customer? The Old Economy executive kept his word—namely, his implicit promise to the audience that he would address the topic listed in the promotional materials for the event. The New Economy executive did not. Instead, he disappointed many members of the paying audience by not living up to his billing.

Going forward, all of us in business would do well to remember two things. First, the Internet and digital technologies are here to stay. Second, so are the people who hype them. That said, let's focus the majority of our time on developing practical applications for the first, and spend significantly less time listening to the second.

ABOUT THE AUTHOR

Brian Ross works at a Fortune 500 company, where he is a manager on the e-commerce team. He lives far away from Silicon Valley in a less hyped part of the world. *When the Caffeine Wears Off* is his first book.